YORK NOTES

General Editors: Professor A.N. Jeffares (*University of Stirling*) & Professor Suheil Bushrui (*American University of Beirut*)

Thomas Hardy

SELECTED POEMS

Notes by Roger Elliott

MA MLITT (OXFORD) MED (WALES)
Lecturer in English, United Nations Institute for Namibia

LONGMAN
YORK PRESS

YORK PRESS
Immeuble Esseily, Place Riad Solh, Beirut

LONGMAN GROUP LIMITED
Longman House, Burnt Mill, Harlow,
Essex CM20 2JE, England
Associated companies, branches and representatives
throughout the world

First published 1982
Tenth impression 1994

ISBN 0-582-78294-5

Produced by Longman Singapore Publishers Pte Ltd
Printed in Singapore

Contents

Part 1

Introduction

THOMAS HARDY was born on 2 June 1840 in the small village of Higher Bockhampton, close to Dorchester, the county town of Dorset. Queen Victoria had been on the throne for three years and the Industrial Revolution was well under way in the north and midlands of England; but Dorset, in the west of the country, was hardly affected yet by the great industrial upheaval. It was an agricultural region of villages and small market towns with a pattern of life that had changed very little for centuries. Hardy's father was a self-employed mason, living in the large cottage that his grandfather had built around 1800. This meant the Hardys were of the cottager class of craftsmen and traders who served the farming community. Unlike the farm labourer, who in the Dorset of the 1840s was a national byword for poverty, the cottager enjoyed a fair amount of independence in his leased cottage and tended to have sufficient money and leisure to act as the cultural leader of the folk community. The Hardys, for instance, were the backbone of the village choir which played and sang in church and at village festivities and parties.

Hardy was the eldest of four children, two boys and two girls. His father seems to have been an easy-going man who loved music and taught his eldest son to play the violin at an early age; as Hardy grew up he increasingly accompanied his father to local parties where they provided the music for the lively country dances. Hardy's mother seems to have been the driving force behind the marriage, a domineering character softened by a strong sense of humour; she was very ambitious for her eldest son and encouraged him in his early reading. Hardy's love for his parents and relatives is evident in several poems, such as 'The Self-Unseeing' and 'One We Knew'. It was a stable family and a rich environment for a future novelist and poet; both of Hardy's parents were a fund of old tales, folk-songs and ballads, and his paternal grandmother's memory reached back to the French Revolution and Napoleon's threatened invasion of England. She died when Hardy was seventeen, and he later wrote the poem 'One We Knew' about her:

With cap-framed face and long gaze into the embers—
    We seated around her knees—
She would dwell on such dead themes, not as one who remembers,
    But rather as one who sees.

Many of Hardy's poems and stories had their source around the fire in the cottage at Bockhampton.

Hardy possessed a remarkable memory and powers of visual recall that enabled him throughout his long life to draw on early experiences. For instance, when he was about six years old he one day lay on his back among dense ferns feeling as though he never wished to grow up. He recalled the incident in his novel *Jude the Obscure* (1896) and several poems written at different times in his life, 'For Life I Had Never Cared Greatly', 'Childhood Among the Ferns' and 'He Never Expected Much'. The latter was written some eighty years after the event:

> Well, World, you have kept faith with me,
>   Kept faith with me;
> Upon the whole you have proved to be
>   Much as you said you were.
> Since as a child I used to lie
> Upon the leaze and watch the sky,
> Never, I own, expected I
>   That life would all be fair.

This incident suggests that although his childhood may have been happy, he developed his sombre, serious temperament early in life. This was probably partly due to his abnormal sensitivity to suffering. Like Jude in *Jude the Obscure* it pained him to see trees cut, and he was haunted by the memory of a bird he picked up one bitterly cold winter's day, as light as a feather, all skin and bone, starved to death. Some of the stories his elders told him were deeply disturbing to someone of his temperament:

> My father saw four men hung for *being with* some others who had set fire to a rick. Among them was a stripling of a boy of eighteen. Skinny. Half-starved. So frail, so underfed, that they had to put weights on his feet to break his neck. He had rushed to the scene to see the blaze. . . . Nothing my father ever said to me drove the tragedy of life so deeply into my mind.*

In his youth he saw two people hanged, and as a child he knew a sheep-keeping boy who died of starvation. Suffering was nearer home, too. His mother had been a pauper child and in domestic service, and, as Hardy wrote, she had seen 'some very stressful experiences of which she could never speak in her maturer years without pain . . .'.† Hardy's many close

---

*Reported by Hardy's friend Norman Flower, *Just As It Happened*, Cassell, London, 1950, p.92.
†F. E. Hardy, *The Life of Thomas Hardy*, Macmillan, London, 1970, p.8. This is an autobiography written as if by his second wife, Florence. It is cited in these notes as *The Life*.

relatives were mainly of the craftsman class but they seldom seem to have prospered like his father. The prospects for business failure were grim—descent to the wretched condition of the labourer, emigration to a new colony, or movement to an industrial centre. One of Hardy's uncles was a farm labourer who probably emigrated to Australia.

Hardy was an intelligent child and his parents were determined to give him the best education they could afford in those days before education was free. He started school in Lower Bockhampton but soon moved to a larger school in Dorchester where he gained a good basic education. He had to leave at the age of sixteen because his parents could no longer afford to keep him in school and he had to start earning a living. He always regretted that he had not had the chance to go to university but he continued to educate himself with great energy. He began work by being apprenticed to John Hicks, a Dorchester architect and church restorer. As he wrote, his life now became 'twisted of three strands—the professional life, the scholar's life, and the rustic life, combined in the twenty-four hours of one day...'. He began at six in the morning reading the classical authors or the Greek Testament, spent the main part of the day on Gothic architecture, and then often rushed off to play at a 'wedding, christening, or Christmas party in a remote dwelling among the fallow fields ...' (*The Life*, p.32).

Hardy proved an apt pupil to John Hicks and at the age of twenty-two he set off to London to enlarge his experience as an architect, buying a return ticket in case he failed to make his way in the capital. He never needed it as he was fortunate enough to find a place in the office of the fashionable architect, Arthur Bloomfield. However, architecture did not satisfy him as a profession and his thoughts were increasingly turned towards literature. His first interest in writing can be seen in the delightful Wordsworthian poem 'Domicilium', written before he was twenty. In London he set himself a massive course in reading English poetry and wrote many poems himself. Some of these early poems survive and were included in the volumes of verse that he published later in his life, but at the time of writing them he could find no editor interested in publishing them. This is hardly surprising as they must have appeared fairly outlandish at that date. This was a period when Tennyson (1809–92) was popular and Swinburne (1837–1909) was the sensational new poet. Tennyson's poetry is characterised by graceful, mellifluous rhythms and his subjects were often self-consciously romantic, such as the mythical stories of the Arthurian knights. Swinburne, on the other hand, shocked the establishment with his violently atheistic poems; but his verse also is very fluid, hypnotic even in the effect of its surging rhythms. Nothing could be further from this confident, incantatory style than the type of poetry that Hardy was offering to editors. Right from the start he found the essence of his characteristic poetic voice—reticent, hesitant, sometimes deliberately awkward in rhythm and diction. His subject-matter was often starkly contemporary in its concern with the undermining of religious faith by scientific discoveries. The editors of the 1860s were not ready for this new poetic voice.

This was probably a great blow to Hardy, who was faced with the choice of either abandoning literature altogether as a career and concentrating on architecture, or seeing if he could earn a living by writing novels rather than poetry. He chose the latter course, succeeded in it, and thus first made his reputation as a novelist. It should not be forgotten, however, that he began writing poetry before he wrote a novel; and although during the thirty years of his career as a novelist most of his energies went into prose, he never entirely stopped writing poetry. He always regarded himself first and foremost as a poet and not as a novelist. In his opinion, poetry was the highest form of literature. This is not to say that he despised novel-writing, though he sometimes made disparaging remarks about it in order to shift the emphasis on to his poetic achievement. It is clear that he took novel-writing with the greatest artistic seriousness; as can be seen by the extent of his revisions and acute sensitivity to criticism. His achievement in both forms, the novel and the poem, is generally regarded as of the highest order; so it seems fruitless to debate at which he excelled, when he excelled at both.

London was not good for Hardy's health and in 1867 he returned to Dorchester to work for his old employer, John Hicks. It was here that he began writing his first novel, a social satire called *The Poor Man and the Lady*, which never found a publisher. Around this time he fell in love with his cousin, Tryphena Sparks. The claim that they had an illegitimate child is based on no real evidence, but they were probably engaged to be married. Then, in March 1870, Hardy met the woman who was to eclipse Tryphena. He travelled to St Juliot Church, near Boscastle in northern Cornwall, to attend to some restoration work; and there, amid the spectacular scenery of the region, he met his future wife, Emma Lavinia Gifford, the rector's sister-in-law. Their courtship lasted four years, during which time Hardy established his career as a novelist, publishing his first novel *Desperate Remedies* in 1871, the pastoral *Under the Greenwood Tree* in 1872, *A Pair of Blue Eyes* in 1873, and *Far From the Madding Crowd* in 1874. The latter was a popular and critical success, and on the strength of this Hardy married Emma in 1874 and abandoned architecture altogether to concentrate on writing.

For the next eleven years Hardy and his wife lived in a variety of homes in Dorset and London until they settled in Dorchester in 1885 at Max Gate, the house that Hardy designed for himself. Between 1870 and 1896 Hardy wrote thirteen novels, the most notable of which are: *Far from the Madding Crowd* (1874), *The Return of the Native* (1878), *The*

Trumpet-Major (1880), *The Mayor of Casterbridge* (1886), *The Wood-landers* (1887), *Tess of the D'Urbervilles* (1889) and *Jude the Obscure* (1896). Many of the themes in these novels recur in his poetry and illustrate the social background against which the poems were written. The novels are generally tragic in outlook, focusing on the thwarted love and aspirations of that rural class of cottagers to which Hardy belonged by birth. Because Hardy was born in an isolated, rural area he was in a position to witness the old village community as it had been with little change for centuries; and then to witness the breakdown of this community during the course of his lifetime when even remote areas such as Dorset underwent radical changes. It was the cottager class which suffered most from these changes. Labourers' wages and living conditions were greatly improved compared with the starvation levels of the 1840s, especially after unionisation in the 1870s, but there was less of a place in the improved agricultural economy for the independent cottager. As Hardy observed in *Tess of the D'Urbervilles* (1889), the landowners, extending and consolidating their property into larger, more economic farms, resented the cottagers' independence and needed their small holdings and cottages for their own use. When the cottagers became dispossessed they sank, like Tess, to the level of labourers; or, like Jude, they drifted into the towns. The dispossession of the cottagers led to the breakdown of the village culture they had led, and the process was exacerbated by the labourers exercising their newly-found economic strength by migrating from one farm to another instead of remaining in the same village all their lives. Continuity and traditions were lost in the villages and the old way of life steadily died. Hardy himself had risen above this in class terms because of his artistic and financial success, but he witnessed the changes and, while never sentimentalising the harsher aspects of the old village culture, he mourned the passing of many of its good aspects in his novels and poems. Often his poems recount the old way of life with nostalgic affection and little overt comment, as in 'The Choirmaster's Burial', 'Winter Night in Woodland' and the numerous ballads dealing with the superstitious exploits of the local 'Quire', such as 'The Paphian Ball'. More poignantly, there are those poems such as 'The Oxen' and 'Afternoon Service at Mellstock' which reveal the tension between his emotional sympathy with the way of life into which he was born, and his sense of alienation from that way of life through social changes, both in his personal life and in society in general.

Hardy was socially separated from the class to which he felt emotionally attached and he recorded its destruction and his own tensions in his writing. These tensions were not only due to socio-economic forces in his personal life and society at large, but were also due to intellectual changes that occurred in his lifetime. Charles Darwin's (1809–82) *Origin of Species* was published in 1859 and prompted a debate on the relationship between scientific discoveries and religious faith. Hardy was one of the early readers of Darwin and he followed the debate closely. He came to share the view of many intellectuals that the Bible was not infallible: that there was much in it, such as the story of the creation of the world, that was denied by the findings of science. It was not only that certain stories in the Bible seemed false when subjected to scientific inquiry, but that scientific discoveries seemed to replace the Christian man-centred universe ruled by a caring God with a vaster, infinitely older universe, indifferent to mankind and the individual, and ruled by chance or mechanical laws. It was a similar revolution to that brought about by the Copernican discovery in the sixteenth century that the earth is not the centre of the solar system—intellectual fact demanded an emotional adjustment to man's sense of his place in the vast scheme of things.

Hardy lost his faith in Christianity, probably during his years in London or soon after, and he turned to philosophy to discover the meaning of life. But contemporary philosophy tended to join with science in teaching that the world is not a caring, forgiving place but an arena of struggle where only the fittest survive. Hardy came to believe that man, in comparison with the animals, had developed his acute consciousness of suffering by some unfortunate accident of the mechanical processes that govern life. After death comes oblivion, and if a God exists he (or 'it' as Hardy preferred to say) is uncaring and probably lacking in the consciousness that man had accidentally and tragically developed. The anguish and conflicts this view of life caused Hardy are evident in many of his poems. In his last novel, *Jude the Obscure*, it manifests itself as a scathing attack on those people, especially women, who fail to lead their lives by the humane principles dictated by their reason, and retreat into a social conformity that is sanctioned by established religion. One aspect of social conformity that Hardy felt particularly strongly about was the general adherence to what he regarded as an inhumane marriage system that made divorce from an incompatible partner extremely difficult at that time.

There were personal reasons for this dislike of the marriage system. His wife's assistance in copying his manuscripts for the publisher is evident in all his novels until *Jude the Obscure*, and by the 1890s their marriage was unhappy and strained. There were many reasons for this; one, perhaps, was that their marriage was childless. Certainly they had incompatible temperaments. Hardy was initially attracted to Emma by her vivacity and impetuousness, endearing characteristics in a lover but perhaps tiresome to a husband of Hardy's retiring and sombre temperament. From Emma's point of view, Hardy's nature must have been a depressing influence on her natural, careless gaiety. There was also a curious literary rivalry, compounded by class differences. Emma was stoutly middle class and had literary ambitions which were never fulfilled; while her husband concealed his humble origins and moved from literary success to literary success in ever more glittering social circles. Reflected glory was not enough for Emma. Matters were made worse in the 1890s by the series of infatuations which Hardy developed for a series of attractive upper-class ladies of literary pretensions. He lavished attentions on their feeble literary efforts, while ignoring his wife's writing which was not without some real descriptive powers, as is evident from her manuscript *Some Recollections*, published by Oxford University Press in 1979. *Jude the Obscure* was a double blow to Emma in its twin attacks on the institutions of marriage and the Church. The former she took as a searing public attack on herself, the latter insulted her deepest beliefs as she was a devout Christian and devoted to the Church of England.

Jude the Obscure was heavily criticised for its views, accused of obscenity and blasphemy by critics and readers. Hardy, always acutely sensitive to criticism, decided to abandon novel-writing and concentrate on poetry. Perhaps he had said all he could in novel form in the contemporary climate of opinion. *Jude the Obscure* is the most autobiographical of his novels and his involvement in it seems to have been particularly personal. After the attacks on it, he may have felt he could write on subjects that were close to him more easily in the form of poetry. Certainly he had made enough money from his novels by 1896 to have the financial security to devote his attention exclusively to his first love—poetry.

Hardy's turning from prose to poetry cannot have helped the Hardy marriage. The three volumes of poetry published before Emma's death in 1912 consist of philosophical poems revealing an unhappy man, narratives obsessively concerned with unhappy marriages, and lyrics addressed to lovers, relatives or friends but seldom to the poet's wife. Husband and wife continued to live together but hardly spoke to each other; yet Hardy cannot have been unaware that his wife was becoming seriously ill with gall-stones, a lingering and painful disease. Although she suffered for many years from this disease, she died quite suddenly from it in November 1912. Hardy was shocked, surprised and plunged into deep remorse. He expressed his complex and developing reactions to her death in a magnificent series of poems, the 'Poems of 1912–13'. Robert Gittings, in his biography of Hardy,* claims Hardy wrote these poems out of a sense of guilt over his part in their relationship, particularly in his lack of care for her in her last years of pain and in not foreseeing her death. But the remorse in these poems and their range of response is of a much broader nature than this, being directed towards a sense of sorrow that their love which had burned so brightly at first had

* See *The Older Hardy*, Penguin Books, Harmondsworth, 1980, pp.206–7.

perished many years ago and never been rekindled. By her death, Emma seemed to have prevented reconciliation, as the first poem in the series, 'The Going' expresses:

> ... All's past amend,
>   Unchangeable. It must go.
> I seem but a dead man held on end
> To sink down soon. ...

Paradoxically, though, as the later poems in the series reveal, it was by dying that Emma rekindled Hardy's love. Whatever guilt Hardy may have been expiating in these poems, what is impressive about them is the poignant and consoling rediscovery of his lost love.

There was, however, another reason why Hardy might have felt remorseful about Emma's death. While ignoring his wife, he had been devoting his attentions for the past five years to a much younger woman called Florence Dugdale. She was one of his young literary ladies, though she had no aristocratic connections and had been a school-teacher. She had been working as Hardy's secretary for some time and in 1914 she became his wife. She was a great support to Hardy in his old age but the relationship was not always an easy one for her. With a type of irony typical in Hardy's writing, Florence discovered that roles had been reversed. Instead of writing poems to her, Hardy wrote dozens of poems about Emma, whom he had ignored for years while she was alive.

Hardy was aware of the unkind personal trait that led him to ignore the woman he had by his side and dote on one he could not have because she was dead, or married to another, or because he was married himself. It is a subject he treated in its manifold complications in many poems. In 'An Upbraiding', he places accusations against himself in Emma's mouth:

> Now I am dead you sing to me
>   The songs we used to know,
> But while I lived you had no wish
>   Or care for doing so.
>
> Now I am dead you come to me
>   In the moonlight, comfortless;
> Ah, what would I have given alive
>   To win such tenderness!
>
> When you are dead, and stand to me
>   Not differenced, as now,
> But like again, will you be cold
>   As when we lived, or how?

In a very late poem, 'Surview', he accuses himself of failing in his life to practice that charity, or 'loving-kindness' as he often called it, that he movingly teaches in his novels and poems:

> 'You taught not that which you set about,'
>   Said my own voice talking to me;
> 'That the greatest of things is Charity. . . .'

This is the nearest Hardy comes to confessional poetry, distancing himself by biblical language and dialogue; but his honesty, his strict adherence to facts, and his sincerity are salient features of his poetry.

Whatever Hardy's own accusations against himself, 'loving-kindness' is a central feature of his poetry and it is to his poetry that our attention must be directed. In the poem 'In Tenebris II' he called himself one 'Who holds that if way to the Better there be, it exacts a full look at the Worst'. This is a rigorous view but it is not wholly pessimistic. Although he regarded the development of man's consciousness of suffering as a ghastly accident, he believed that it could lead to a better life. Suffering can be alleviated, sometimes even avoided altogether, by developing the spirit of 'loving-kindness'. This spirit should not only be extended between men but from man to animals and even to the whole of nature. Darwin had shown the interrelatedness of all life, animate and inanimate, and Hardy is peculiarly modern in his awareness of the ecological responsibility of man towards the entire natural environment. In his more optimistic mood, he hoped that if mankind developed its awareness and compassionate spirit it might, over the vast span of evolution, pass on this highest form of consciousness to the unconscious creator of the universe. He sometimes called the creator 'the Will', a purposive but unconscious force. He ends his great poetic drama on the Napoleonic wars, *The Dynasts* (1904, 1906 and 1908), on this hopeful note which is called 'evolutionary meliorism'. The Spirit of Pities, the youngest spirit with the most developed consciousness, is speaking:

> But—a stirring thrills the air
> Like to sounds of joyance there
>   That the rages
>   Of the ages
> Shall be cancelled, and deliverance offered from the darts that were,
> Consciousness the Will informing, till It fashion all things fair!

A more distant hope can hardly be imagined and, as 'In Tenebris II' insists, it depends on man avoiding pleasant delusions and facing up to 'the Worst' in life, the evils that must be fought against. Even this faint optimism was severely shaken by the ghastliness of the First World War. Yet, whatever Hardy's philosophical outlook on life, the emphasis on charity and forgiveness remains pervasive throughout his poetry. This clearly comes from his Christian upbringing, and although he lost his faith in the divinity of Christ and his belief in a caring God, much of the spirit of Christ's teaching is to be found in his writing. Perhaps the most characteristic mood of Hardy's poetry is one of gentleness and compassion for suffering.

Hardy published eight volumes of poetry between 1898 and his death in 1928. All of them, especially the earlier and later volumes, contain poems written in his youth and early middle age; but the bulk of his poetry was written in his late fifties and up to his death at the age of eighty-eight. Such an outpouring of poetry from an elderly man is almost unequalled in English literature. One reason for this has already been mentioned: that Hardy had a remarkable ability to recall past events and this provided him with a rich source of inspiration in old age. But the main reason is that the great theme of his poetry is the mutability of life, the tragic contrast between the hopes, joy and love of youth and the loss of love and inevitable decay of old age. The inspiration for the poems arose from the viewpoint on time that he gained through a long life, the lofty perspective of one who has lived for many years.

In the last years of his life Hardy received many honours, the Order of Merit in 1910, followed, to his delight, by honorary doctorates from the universities that he had been too poor to attend as a young man. He became the 'Grand Old Man of Letters', visited by younger writers such as Robert Graves (b.1895), Siegfried Sassoon (1886–1967) and T. E. Lawrence (1888–1935).They admired the extraordinarily modern poetry that this elderly man was writing, one who had listened to Dickens (1812–70) reading one of his novels, who had known Swinburne and dined with Tennyson, Browning (1812–89), Meredith (1828–1909) and Henry James (1843–1916). Hardy was a link with the Victorian Age and yet still, in his eighties, a modern writer. He remained physically and mentally alert, still writing poetry, almost up to the day of his death on 11 January 1928. His ashes are laid in Westminster Abbey and his heart is buried at Stinsford Churchyard by the graves of his parents and first wife.

A note on the text

The eight volumes of poetry that Hardy published are: *Wessex Poems* (1898), *Poems of the Past and Present* (1902), *Time's Laughingstocks* (1909), *Satires of Circumstance* (1914), *Moments of Vision* (1917), *Late Lyrics and Earlier* (1922), *Human Shows* (1925), and *Winter Words* (posthumously in 1928). Between 1902 and 1908 he was working on *The Dynasts*, an epic drama in prose and poetry, published in three parts (1904, 1906 and 1908). Apart from *The Dynasts*, all these poems were brought together in *The Collected Poems of Thomas Hardy*, Macmillan, London, 1930; and this volume was not superseded until James Gibson edited *The Complete Poems of Thomas Hardy* in 1976 as part of the New Wessex Edition of all Hardy's works published by Macmillan, London. This volume contains twenty-seven poems that were not in *The Collected Poems*, including six from *The Dynasts*, and consists of nine hundred and forty-seven poems in all. Although a variorum edition has subsequently been published, *The Complete Poems* is the standard text for anyone who loves Hardy's poetry. Quantity is not necessarily a sign of quality, but the nine hundred and forty-seven poems in this volume provide an inexhaustible store of poetic riches. Hardy was incapable of writing a poem that is not strongly stamped with his personality, and even in those poems that are only partial successes there are moments when Hardy's idiosyncratic poetic voice speaks clearly enough to make them interesting and sometimes moving.

Obviously nine hundred and forty-seven poems of varying quality are far too many for a student coming to the poetry for the first time to digest. A student must begin with a selection, and the best one for the beginner is *Chosen Poems of Thomas Hardy*, edited by James Gibson, Macmillan, London, 1975. This has a straightforward and useful introductory section, a sensible selection of the poems, and a very useful glossary of obscure words after each poem with short but sometimes stimulating notes. If a student learns to appreciate all the poems in this selection, then he or she will be acquainted with most of Hardy's best poems. A few poems not included in *Chosen Poems* are discussed in the course of these notes, notably 'And There Was a Great Calm' and the three 'In Tenebris' poems. Students are strongly advised to read these in *The Complete Poems*, together with the following which also do not appear in *Chosen Poems*: 'Logs on the Hearth', 'Voices from Things Growing in a Churchyard', 'Julie-Jane', 'The Ruined Maid', 'Friends Beyond', 'Wessex Heights', 'A Dream or No', 'The Phantom Horsewoman' and 'The Five Students'.

Details of larger selections of Hardy's poems are given in Part 5 of these notes, and interested students are strongly recommended to turn to *The Complete Poems* once they have mastered the limited selection in *Chosen Poems*.

Part 2

Summaries
of SELECTED POEMS

THESE NOTES on the poems follow the order devised by James Gibson for *Chosen Poems*, beginning with 'Poems Mainly Autobiographical' in broadly chronological order, followed by 'Incidents and Stories' and 'Descriptive and Animal Poems'. It is difficult to know how to group a selection of Hardy's poems and this classification is not wholly satisfactory, but it was decided to follow the order of *Chosen Poems* because this is the text most likely to be used by the student.

Although *Chosen Poems* is a small selection considering Hardy's enormous poetic output, it is still too large for every poem to be dealt with in the limited space available for these notes. Rather than write a very brief note on every poem, it seemed more useful to select thirty and analyse them in some detail. It is hoped that these examples of practical criticism will act as models which the student can apply to the rest of the poems. The criteria for selecting the thirty poems were either that they are generally regarded as Hardy's finest works or that they represent characteristic features of his work, as in 'Snow in the Suburbs' and 'An August Midnight'.

'The Oxen'

This is one of Hardy's most nostalgic and wistful poems. There was an old country legend that at midnight on Christmas Eve the oxen would kneel down in homage to Christ. The first two verses bring us into the rustic, communal society of worshippers seated like a 'flock' around a dying fire. The 'elder' (a word with biblical associations) proclaims the old superstition of the kneeling animals, and among the listeners there is absolute trust in the legend. The third verse shifts the time perspective from the past to the present, stating that few would believe 'So fair a fancy .../In these years'. Notice the heavy pause after the word 'years'. Up to that point the poem has moved with the easy rhythm of the ballad metre, the rhythm of the folk tradition; but this rhythm is interrupted by the modern doubts that have destroyed belief in the legends of this tradition, and, for many, the Christianity that was supported by these legends. The interruption is, however, only a momentary one; the ballad rhythm reasserts itself, flowing on between verses III and IV, as Hardy reasserts the value, if not the truth, of the old legend. He says that if he met an old friend who still believed the legend, he would go with him to the 'barton' by the 'coomb' that they used to know 'Hoping it might be so'.

The pathos of this hope in the truth of an old legend lies in a profound sense of loss that cries out for a comfort that Hardy cannot really permit himself. He knows the superstition is not true, that the animals will not be kneeling, but this factual truth is gained only at the loss of that sense of calm and trust that he shared with the rural community of verses I and II as a child. Such is his sense of loss that he feels he could be tempted to hope for the hopeless, but he has no real expectation that this will bring any consolation.

NOTES AND GLOSSARY:
barton: *(dialect)* farmyard
yonder: *(archaic)* over there
coomb: *(dialect)* valley

'Afternoon Service at Mellstock'

This poem is set at 'Mellstock' Church, Hardy's name for Stinsford Church which he regularly attended as a boy. He describes the scene as it was 'circa 1850' when he was ten years old. The first verse depicts the drowsy, calm group of villagers united in religious worship. The second verse extends the communal unity within the church to a sense of the unity of mankind with nature. The congregation look beyond the church towards natural scenes, and they are themselves like inanimate nature, 'swaying like the trees'. The third verse makes that time shift from the past to the present that is so typical of Hardy's poetic method and perspective on life. The worship in the past was 'mindless' because it was based on faith, intuition and tradition, and not on reason. Yet, for all his subsequent intellectual gains, Hardy is not sure that his life is richer or fuller 'Since we stood psalming there'.

This is a sad comment on his loss of faith in Christianity in the face of intellectual challenges. Yet this loss did not mean a total rejection of Christianity. Although he regarded himself as an agnostic, he also called himself 'Churchy; not in an intellectual sense, but in so far as instincts and emotions ruled' (*The Life*, p.376). He remained true to the spirit of Christianity and deeply attached to the rituals of the Church in which he had been raised, and to the church buildings themselves. But in losing his faith he had lost that instinctive sense of oneness with other men and nature, and that inner peace he had possessed as a child.

NOTES AND GLOSSARY:
panelled pew: large benches in a church with wood panels

Tate-and-Brady psalm: Nahum Tate (1652–1715) and Nicholas Brady
(1659–1726) published a well-known metrical ver-
sion of the Psalms in 1696

'The Self-Unseeing'

This poem describes Hardy's return to his birthplace at Higher
Bockhampton as though he is showing someone round the old cottage.
He points out the footworn floor and the front door which used to be in a
different place when he was a child—ten feet to the left of the present
door as one faces the building. The literal nature of mentioning the
'former door' is typical of Hardy's fascination with fact and interest in
detail. In spite of the risk of banality, it is often effective. In this case it
adds to the suggestion of change which is an essential element of the
poem. Through 'the former door' the 'dead feet walked in'—probably a
reference to Hardy's father who died in 1892. It is not clear who the
people are in the second verse, but they are probably Hardy's mother
sitting in the chair and smiling into the fire, and his father playing the
violin. Hardy is the dancer of the third verse. He describes himself as
'extraordinarily sensitive to music' and as a child he used to dance
ecstatically to hide the tears that music brought to his eyes (*The Life*,
p.15). The day he is describing in the past was blessed with happiness,
'Yet we were looking away!'; the true value of that moment was not
realised by the participants. Contentment and happiness are often not
appreciated at the time but only later by contrast with less happy times.
Like so many of Hardy's poems, this one is nostalgic without being
sentimental. We are convinced by the detail of his recall that he was
genuinely happy at that time, and the sadness at the centre of the poem is
only hinted at in the final line.

The extremely skilful handling of metre and diction is an essential part
of the success of this poem. The poem appears straightforward, as seems
appropriate in a poem of nostalgia for the pleasures of childhood; but
Hardy said he 'loved the art of concealing art' (*The Life*, p.310), and it is
always worthwhile to analyse his 'simple' poems to see how carefully he
directs our responses. Notice the structure: lines 1 and 2 describe the
floor, 3 and 4 describe the door, 5 and 6 describe 'she', 7 and 8 describe
'he'. The main pause comes half-way between each verse at the subject
dividing line. The impression is of an orderly, reminiscent tour round the
cottage. The third verse changes the structure and the rhythm. Each line
is a separate entity, divided by rhythm, punctuation and alliteration
(similar or identical sounds in close proximity—'d's' in line 1, 'b's' in line
2, 'g's' in line 3, 'w's' in line 4). The first three lines have a driving rhythm,
the main stress falling on the first word, elevating the conversational
tones of the first two verses to an almost ecstatic level as Hardy recalls his

happiness. The final line breaks this rhythm, stressing the second word in the line. This changes the mood from an assertive major one to a meditative minor mood which reflects its sadness over the whole poem.

NOTES AND GLOSSARY:
Bowing: playing a violin with a bow
emblazoned: coloured with bright, joyful emotions

'Neutral Tones'

This poem opens by describing two lovers standing by a pond in winter. In the second verse, their few words only lessen their love for each other, and in the third verse the woman's attempt to smile only reflects her lack of joy, the smile turning into a bitter grimace which is 'ominous' because it signals their future separation. The two middle verses express extremely well those reticent, minimal actions that can indicate faltering love, but the greatest achievement of the poem lies in the first and last verses which frame the middle ones. The first verse describes the scene, evoking a sense of desolation through natural imagery that reflects the state of their love. It is winter when all nature seems dead; even the usual fiery sun is pale, like the dying fire of their love. A few grey leaves lie on the ground, fallen from an ash tree and suggesting again an extinguished fire. There is no warm colour in the picture, everything is in the 'neutral tones' of white and grey. Although this verse powerfully evokes a mood, it is only in the final verse when the images are repeated, together with the girl's face described in the middle verses, that the images become explicitly symbolic. The 'ominous' has been fulfilled—their love has died. The description of nature in the first verse, and the one of her face, are 'shaped' into permanent symbols of the pain of lost love. This particular scene has come, through the power of Hardy's memory, to stand as a symbol for a particular emotion. The emotion is a commonly experienced one, and thus Hardy has transmuted a personal event into a symbol for a universal emotion. This is typical of Hardy's poetic method at its best, and since this poem was written as early as 1867, it shows how quickly he matured as a poet.

The diction is simple and stark as befits the subject of the poem, but notice how subtly the rhythm is used. For instance, the last two lines have a weight and solemnity achieved by the main stresses falling heavily on each of the objects symbolising the loss of love in the penultimate line, and an extra foot being added to lengthen the final line (it has four stresses whereas the final lines of verses I–III have only three).

NOTES AND GLOSSARY:
chidden: *(literary)* rebuked or scolded

starving sod: a rare meaning of 'starving' is to suffer from or perish with the cold. The 'sod' means the turf, the grassy upper layer of earth

'Great Things'

The joys in this poem are of drinking cider, dancing and love, but such is Hardy's temperament that he cannot celebrate life's joys without considering its sorrows as well. The first three verses describing the joys have an easy, swinging rhythm with chiming internal rhymes in the third lines. In the last verse, the rhythm breaks down into a more hesitant, halting form as Hardy questions the validity of the joys in the face of death. But after the question 'What then?' in the fifth line, followed by a heavy pause as we await the answer, the poem recaptures its confident rhythm as Hardy affirms that the joys of life are still 'Great things' in spite of their ephemeral nature.

NOTES AND GLOSSARY:
cyder: an alcoholic drink made from the juice of apples, more commonly spelt 'cider'
Spinning down to Weymouth town/By Ridgeway thirstily: Hardy enjoyed the new pastime of cycling and used to cycle down the 'Ridgeway' road to Weymouth, seven miles south of Max Gate
lea: a large grassy field
flings: dances

'When I Set Out for Lyonnesse'

This poem records Hardy's first visit to St Juliot in Cornwall in March 1870 when he fell in love with Emma Gifford. 'Lyonnesse' is Hardy's name for that area of northern Cornwall that is romantically associated with the Arthurian legends, St Juliot being close to Tintagel Castle which may have been one of King Arthur's strongholds. The journey from Dorchester to this remote region was a difficult one in 1870 and Hardy had to begin before dawn, as the first verse records. From the start, the journey was associated with romance and adventure in the mind of the young poet, and it is clear, even without biographical knowledge of his life, that he fell in love at 'Lyonnesse'. The experience of new love drew from Hardy a lyric that is uncharacteristically buoyant, vigorous and musical. The form he uses is a type of Rondel, very appropriate for celebrating the wonder and mystery of new love with its chiming rhyme scheme and ringing repetitions.

NOTES AND GLOSSARY:
The rime was on the spray: frost was on the branches of trees and shrubs
bechance: happen
sojourn: *(archaic)* make a temporary stay
durst: dared
wizard: the legendary wizard Merlin is said to have been a member of King Arthur's court and Cornwall has always been associated with magic

---

'The Last Signal'

This poem is dedicated to the Dorset poet and scholar, William Barnes (1801–86), who was a friend of Hardy's and a close neighbour after Hardy moved to Max Gate. It recounts an actual incident that occurred when Hardy was walking from Max gate to the churchyard where Barnes was to be buried. The setting sun reflected from Barnes's distant coffin a flash of light against the dark east sky, 'As with a wave of his hand'. The poem is very characteristic of Hardy, not only in its familiar churchyard setting, but in the extreme simplicity of the event and the plainness of its expression which is nevertheless charged with a sense of sadness. It possesses that typically restrained sense of all having been said that can possibly be said in a world that promises no hereafter and where human affections are precious but painfully transient. The significance of the event lies on the plane of human pathos. There is no spiritual significance in a wave that is only 'As' a wave in the mind of a sorrowing friend.

NOTES AND GLOSSARY:
abode: *(archaic)* home
yew-boughed: beneath the boughs of yew-trees; the yew, an evergreen tree that lives to a great age, is often planted in grave-yards
livid: of a bluish, leaden colour

'A Broken Appointment'

The occasion of this poem was probably the failure of Florence Henniker, a literary lady with whom Hardy fell in love in the 1890s, to keep an appointment with him. However, the biographical details are of little importance as the experience is common enough and Hardy consciously transcends the personal element to draw a general moral from the incident. It is a potentially self-pitying poem but Hardy raises it above this level by grieving not for himself but for the woman who has failed to show that 'high compassion' which for 'pure lovingkindness' sake' might have prompted her to keep the appointment. A sense of Time as a destructive force pervades the poem. The 'marching Time' that draws on in verse I is the literal time up to the 'hope-hour' of their appointment. The time-scale in verse II is broader. The poet is a 'time-torn man' and his love is, by implication, younger. As Samuel Hynes points out, by failing to keep the appointment she falls in league with 'Time-the-destroyer, Hardy's old enemy'.*

The main focus of the poem, however, is not on time but on the woman's lack of compassion. Self-pity is avoided by the oblique way in which Hardy makes the complaint. The diction is simple enough but the syntax is convoluted, especially the second sentence where the main clause 'Grieved I' is withheld in such a way that his personal hurt is transferred into a more generalised statement about unselfishness. The difficulty the reader is likely to encounter on first reading this sentence is deliberately designed to throw the emphasis on his moral-philosophical reflections rather than on his private hurt. On the other hand, each verse is framed by the repetition of the first line in the last line, 'You did not come', and 'You love not me'. This reintroduces the poet in his loneliness in a poignant manner, fusing general reflection with personal sadness. It is a superbly well controlled poem.

NOTES AND GLOSSARY:

make: character
the hope-hour stroked its sum: the clock struck the longed-for hour of their appointment

---

'The Impercipient'

Like 'The Oxen' and 'Afternoon Service at Mellstock', this poem arises out of Hardy's conflicting attitudes towards religion. 'The Impercipient' means one who cannot see. Hardy is 'At a Cathedral Service', surrounded by Christian believers, but he cannot himself see what they see, share their faith. Being, as he said, 'churchy', he frequently attended Christian services throughout his life although he was agnostic. This poem expresses the painful sense of isolation he felt among 'comrades' who had retained a faith that he had lost. He is denied the 'joys' and 'ease' of their faith. He feels no arrogance at perhaps possessing a truer, more intellectually sound view of life; on the contrary, he finds his inability to believe a painful 'mystery' and wonders whether it is due to some 'lack' in himself. The last two lines of verse III criticise the faithful for failing to show him the charity they profess as Christians:

*In *The Pattern of Hardy's Poetry*, University of North Carolina Press, Chapel Hill, 1961, p.127.

My lack might move their sympathies
    And Christian charity!

Instead, as the final verse makes clear, the faithful charge him with actually wanting the hopeful message of Christianity to be untrue. This he denies with the anguished metaphor in which he compares himself to a bird with clipped wings:

O, doth a bird deprived of wings
    Go earth-bound wilfully!

The two final lines control the emotional outburst with a resolve towards stoical calm.

NOTES AND GLOSSARY:

band:	the congregation worshipping in the cathedral
Shining Land:	heaven
infelicity:	unhappiness
wind-swept pine:	the sound of the wind in the pine is similar to the sound of the sea. The believers think they hear 'the glorious distant sea'—a metaphor for heaven. Hardy, from his scientific materialist point of view, cannot share the distant vision but feels the sound is only the wind in a nearby pine tree
meet:	*(biblical)* appropriate
liefer:	*(rare)* gladly

'Drummer Hodge'

Hardy wrote a number of poems about the Boer War (1899–1902), fought between Britain and the Boers (South Africans of Dutch descent). This poem is an elegy for a Wessex drummer-boy who was killed during the war. Hardy calls him 'Hodge' which was the common nickname for a West country labourer and was associated, as Hardy said, with a 'being of uncouth manner and aspect, stolid understanding, and snail-like movement'.* Hardy protested against this stereotype, insisting that the labourers were all individuals, 'men of many minds, infinite in difference'.† This poem extends the protest to the carelessness with which the lives of ordinary people are treated in war. The young drummer is buried with no ceremony, 'thrown' into his grave 'Uncoffined—just as found'. The strangeness of the scene is emphasised by the Boer words for the un-English countryside—'kopje-crest', the

---

* Harold Orel, 'The Dorsetshire Labourer', *Thomas Hardy's Personal Writing*, Macmillan, London, 1967, p.168.
† ibid., pp.170–1.

'veldt'. Foreign constellations wheel above the grave. The second verse expresses Hodge's sense of bewilderment in this strange land of the 'Karoo' and the 'Bush'. Yet, in the third verse Hodge becomes a part of this foreign landscape. It is as though he has transcended the demeaning significance attached to his life by his death which has transformed him into part of an eternal, creative and mysterious process. He will be a 'portion' of that land for ever, and life, in the form of a tree, will spring from his death. The constellations and stars that emphasised his ignorance and loneliness in verses I and II, become one with him in this cosmic process and 'reign/His stars eternally'. Hardy celebrates this eternal cycle in another fine poem, 'Voices from Things Growing in a Churchyard'.

NOTES AND GLOSSARY:

kopje-crest:	crest of an outcrop of rock
veldt:	open grassland
Karoo:	arid uplands
Bush:	shrubby, uncultivated land
loam:	fertile soil of clay and sand
gloam:	evening twilight

'The Man He Killed'

This is another poem of protest written during the Boer War. When it was first published in *Harper's Weekly* in 1902, there was this headnote: 'Scene: the settle of the Fox Inn, Stagfoot Lane. Characters: the speaker (a returned soldier) and his friends, natives of the hamlet.' The Fox Inn is in a village a few miles from Dorchester. The returned soldier is discussing the man he had killed during the war. He is puzzled by the inhumanity of war. If he had met the man in peace they would have enjoyed drinking together, but in the situation of war they tried to kill each other. The soldier's stumbling attempts to explain this are well conveyed by the broken rhythms of verse III where he clings, in some desperation, to the impersonal label of 'foe' given to the man he killed. He cannot, however, rest content with this stereotype; he cannot help seeing the man as a human-being like himself who probably became involved in a meaningless war for the same reasons. The soldier is baffled by the inhumane situation in which you kill a man for whom, in other circumstances, you would gladly buy a drink or to whom you would give some money. The soldier's conclusion, 'quaint and curious war is!', is so inadequate that it only further reflects his confusion. The achievement of the poem lies partly in its restraint. Hardy makes no overt comment; war is condemned by the inability of a humane man to explain the inhumane act he was forced to perform in its name.

NOTES AND GLOSSARY:

to wet:	to drink
nipperkin:	a small measure of spirits
'list:	enlist in the army
off-hand:	carelessly
traps:	belongings
half-a-crown:	an old unit of money, equal to $12\frac{1}{2}$ pence

---
'The Darkling Thrush'

This poem is set on the last day of December 1900 and was first called 'By
the Century's Deathbed'. It is the depth of winter, colourless, frosty and
grey. The scene is similar to that of 'Neutral Tones': desolate and devoid
of human life. The second verse explicitly compares the dead-looking
landscape with the past century, stretched out like a corpse. Life appears
to be negated, and 'every spirit upon earth' as 'fervourless' as the poet.
On this desolate scene breaks the beautiful song of the thrush:

> In a full-hearted evensong
> Of joy illimited.

It seems an inexplicable act of courage for the 'frail, gaunt, and small'
bird 'to fling his soul/Upon the growing gloom'. It is so inexplicable that
Hardy is led to wonder if the bird has access to some source of hopeful
knowledge denied to him:

> Some blessed Hope, whereof he knew
> And I was unaware.

The poem is based upon an ironic contrast between the negative scene
of the first two verses and the bird's joyful song that in the last two verses
suggests the possibility of hope. The strangeness of the contrast suggests
to Hardy that there might be hope; but the poem remains on a level of
suggestion and not of affirmation. The pathos of the poem lies in
Hardy's reticent movement towards acknowledging the possibility of
hope in a world of death, a yearning to recognise and share the bird's
apparent hope coupled with an inability to do so.

NOTES AND GLOSSARY:

Darkling:	shrouded in darkness
coppice:	small wood, grown for cutting
The weakening eye of day:	the pale sun setting below the horizon
bine-stems:	stems of climbing plants like the woodbine
lyres:	old stringed musical instruments
outleant:	stretched out
illimited:	unlimited

'The Convergence of the Twain'

The occasion of this poem was the sinking of the liner *Titanic* on 15 April 1912 on her maiden voyage from Southampton to New York. The *Titanic* was the largest and most opulent liner of its age. She was supposed to be unsinkable and so it was not thought necessary to carry sufficient lifeboats for all those on board. When she struck a huge iceberg at 2 a.m. and began to sink, there were two thousand three hundred and forty people on board of whom one thousand six hundred and thirty-five drowned in the icy water. In his poem, Hardy chose not to focus on the human tragedy of the event but on its philosophical implications. His thoughts were similar to those expressed in *The Times* leader two days after the sinking:

> We build these astounding monsters of steel, fit them up with a luxury beyond the dreams of a Roman Emperor, fill them with a population of thousands, and send them out with the utmost confidence to cross the waters. ... And, then, Nature, the silent, the inscrutable, having submitted to all this mastery, just puts out her finger; and at her touch man is reduced to a helpless pigmy and all his works are swallowed up into nothingness. She does it in her own way, unseen and unforeseen, as though in derision. ... The *Titanic*—the greatest thing we have yet produced—lies at the bottom of the ocean, a useless mass of lumber.
>
> (*The Times*, 17 April 1912).

The poem is divided into two parts. The first five verses describe the sunken ship, contrasting her opulence, her intended purpose to pander to luxury and the 'Pride of Life that planned her', with her fate at the bottom of the ocean, in darkness amid grotesque and slimy sea-creatures. The 'moon-eyed fishes' ask 'What does this vaingloriousness down here?'. The rest of the poem answers the question, presenting a deterministic view of the event. Hardy's 'Immanent Will' is a mysterious life-force that governs the universe. He usually describes it as an unconscious, uncaring force, but in this poem it seems to act with conscious intent to punish man for his pride in building the enormous and boastfully-proclaimed 'unsinkable' ship. It 'Prepared a sinister mate'; as they grew separately, one made by man, the other a natural growth, they were destined to be brought together. The 'Spinner of the Years' is a form of fate which brings them together in a disastrous 'consummation' of their destiny. It is depicted as a type of marriage, but an unnatural and violent one from which comes not life but death.

NOTES AND GLOSSARY:
Twain: *(archaic)* two
pyres: furnaces for the ship's engines

salamandrine:	the lizard-like animal called the salamandar is said in legend to live in fire
thrid:	*(archaic)* thread through
glass:	reflect
cleaving wing:	the ship cleaves or parts the sea as a bird's wings part the air in flight
anon:	soon

'The Going'

This is the first of the 'Poems of 1912–13', a group of twenty-one poems concerned with Hardy's reaction to his first wife's death in November 1912. We shall consider six of them. 'The Going' appropriately begins the group as it is about Hardy's sense of shock immediately after Emma's death. She died 'calmly, as if indifferent quite', indifferent to life and to her husband's feelings:

Never to bid goodbye
Or lip me the softest call.

Hardy is shocked that there was no chance for a farewell or reconciliation, and numbed by his ignorance that her 'great going/Had place that moment' and 'altered all'. The third verse hints at the development we shall see in this group of poems towards a poetic re-establishment of contact between Hardy and his dead wife; but at this stage it is only the common experience of missing a familiar person who has gone and 'for a breath' thinking you have seen her. The shattering of illusion brings a sense of complete despair at the end of verse III. In verse IV, Hardy momentarily escapes from this despair by recollecting scenes from their early love in Cornwall, a process that is later to become the main source of his consolation. At this stage, the recollections are only able to bring temporary consolation which is followed by bitter remorse at the irrevocably lost opportunity of renewing their love by revisiting the places of their courtship. In its context as words that can never now be spoken, the colloquial tone of the end of verse V is particularly poignant. The final verse continues the colloquial tone, but with a breakdown of rhythm reflecting Hardy's full realisation of the present situation:

Well, Well! All's past amend,
Unchangeable. It must go.

In a remarkable image, Hardy describes himself as already dead, merely held up vertically by his physical body but doomed 'to sink down soon' into his grave. The sense of weary resignation in this verse is then shattered by the despairing cry of anguish in the final sentence. Nothing is resolved, but the poem has explored a large range of the emotional responses and conflicts that Hardy experienced on Emma's death, and has touched on the means whereby he is to find consolation in later poems.

NOTES AND GLOSSARY:
red-veined rocks far West: the rocks and cliffs around St Juliot
rode: Emma used to ride her horse along the cliff-tops
beetling: overhanging in a threatening manner
Beeny Crest: a massive cliff near St Juliot
reining: stopping the horse by pulling on the reins

'The Haunter'

This poem takes us beyond the despair and crowded emotions of immediate bereavement in 'The Going', towards the establishment of the process by which Hardy found consolation. The speaker this time is Emma, and although the psychological impetus of the poem lies in Hardy's imagining that Emma still cares for him, the theme of the poem is their lack of communication. He depicts Emma's ghost lovingly haunting him but perplexed by the problem of letting him know that she does so. There is a strong element of self-reproach in verse II: that he used to ignore her when she could have been a living companion to him. The third verse suggests Hardy's loneliness and reflective nature in the places he visits, always accompanied by Emma's unseen ghost. In the final verse Emma implores that somehow communication must be established between them; but clearly by imagining that her ghost is deeply concerned with his peace of mind, Hardy is already building up towards that consoling communication we witness in later poems.

NOTES AND GLOSSARY:
old aisles: the divisions of a church

'The Voice'

In 'The Haunter', Emma complains that she is:

> Always lacking the power to call to him,
>   Near as I reach thereto.

'The Voice', a far more intense and urgent poem, answers 'The Haunter', as it is about Hardy hearing Emma's 'call'. It begins with the certainty that Emma is calling to him, passionately affirmed by the repeated 'call to me, call to me'. The verse consists of one very complex sentence, reflecting in its reticent obliqueness the painful nature of its subject, and perhaps intended to disguise Hardy's implied criticism of Emma. She had changed during her lifetime from the woman he originally loved, 'the one who was all to me'; but after her death she says she has changed back, 'as at first, when our day was fair'. The second verse expresses something like astonishment that he is really hearing her, 'Can it be you that I hear?'. As if eager to test his perceptions, he moves from hearing to sight, 'Let me view you, then'. Through the power of his memory, he sees her as she used to be when they were young lovers, 'Even to the original air-blue gown!'. The detail of this recall seems to verify its actuality, but the next verse brings doubts. Is he deceived by the wind, is the sight of her to be lost for ever, the sound of her to be 'Heard no more again far or near'? The anguish of these despairing thoughts is continued in the final doubt-ridden verse, and reflected by the complete breakdown of the metre. The leaves falling and the 'Wind oozing thin through the thorn from norward' suggest death and despair, and yet the poem is not totally without hope. Although he is 'faltering', he is still moving 'forward', and the woman is still calling. Hardy shunned illusions and tried to face the 'Worst', but by the same token he was sincere to his feelings and perceptions, and in his mind he can see the woman and she is calling. It is a poem full of anguished conflict about the nature of the reality he perceives; nevertheless it tentatively moves forward towards the consoling vision he was eventually to achieve.

NOTES AND GLOSSARY:

mead: (*poetic*) meadow, grassland that is well watered and often flooded

---

'At Castle Boterel'

In the series 'Poems of 1912–13', 'At Castle Boterel' comes after the poem 'After a Journey' and not, as in Gibson's *Chosen Poems of Thomas Hardy*, before it. It is best to keep to Hardy's original order and read 'After a Journey' before 'At Castle Boterel' because 'After a Journey' ends on an almost ecstatic note of affirmation which is unusual in Hardy and never again attained in this context, whereas 'At Castle Boterel' ends on a mood of sad acquiescence that is characteristic of Hardy and which comes appropriately at the end of the series.

'Castle Boterel' is Hardy's name for Boscastle, the small harbour town near St Juliot, which he revisited in 1913. This visit reawakened memories of 1870 when he climbed the steep hill there with Emma. The power of his memory calls up this scene from the past so that it seems more real than the present. The dreariness of the present is suggested by the rain, but what he sees on the hill is himself and Emma in 'dry March weather'. His memories evoke a complex of emotions that are more measured and balanced than the mood of remorseful anguish in 'The Going' or the near ecstacy he experienced on first rediscovering their 'olden haunts' in 'After a Journey'. Verse III says that what they talked of and did 'matters not much' because love, the 'Something that life will not be balked of', is a common enough experience. Yet, although his experience is just one of millions, it is the most valuable experience possible because it represents feeling and hope in life. To him that moment on the hill is qualitatively of more value than any other 'In that hill's story', and the 'Primaeval rocks' record only one thing—'that we two passed'. This well conveys his sense of the preciousness of that moment, but it is balanced by an appreciation that the value he ascribes to the moment is a purely personal one, 'To one mind never', 'And to me'. The sixth verse accepts Emma's death in her 'substance' but asserts his power to keep her alive in memory. In this sense he can defeat 'Time's unflinching rigour', but the defeat can only be partial because he himself, with his memories, will die. The last verse suggests that his death will come soon, 'my sand is sinking'. The verse is a complex of past, present and future which works on two levels, a literal and a metaphorical one. On the literal level, in the present, he is travelling away from the hill, 'amid the rain', mourning the fact that he is too old to revisit the places he associates with love, 'old love's domain'. This present is interfused with the past; his focus is on the 'phantom figure' of Emma which he sees 'shrinking, shrinking' as he looks back. She represents love to him and he fears that because of his age he is looking on love 'For the very last time'. The 'old love's domain' that he will not 'traverse' again is not only the physical region around Boscastle but also the emotional experience of love. The poem ends with him accepting his coming death.

NOTES AND GLOSSARY:

waggonette: open four-wheeled carriage with facing side-seats
benighted: overtaken by night
chaise: open four-wheeled carriage
Primaeval: as old as the beginning of the world
Time's unflinching rigour,/In mindless rote: Time moves on steadily and relentlessly despite man's feelings, operating in a mechanical, repetitive manner
my sand is sinking: the image is of an hour-glass in which the sand has almost run through to the bottom of the glass

---

'After a Journey'

In March 1913, Hardy revisited the region of Cornwall where he first met and courted Emma. This poem reflects the intensity of the experience and the consolation it brought. The poem is a monologue addressed to the 'voiceless' but nevertheless very real presence of Emma. On returning to her 'olden haunts' there is no longer any doubt in his mind about the reality of his memories, which are so powerful that he feels Emma's presence leading him on in what is almost a trance. He sees her with vivid particularity:

> Facing round about me everywhere,
>   With your nut-coloured hair,
> And grey eyes, and rose-flush coming and going.

The experience of being in the grip of an overwhelming force of memory that takes control of the present is at first bewildering and painful; he is 'lonely, lost' and awed. The second verse lowers the tension by its more conversational tone, but the rhythm becomes more hesitant as though Hardy is finding difficulty in putting his thoughts about their estranged past into words. Hardy wonders what Emma must think of their past, apportioning no blame to either side but describing their division in natural terms, 'Summer gave us sweets, but autumn wrought division'. Death has brought the estrangement to an end, paradoxically bringing a type of reconciliation, 'But all's closed now, despite Time's derision'. In the third verse, Hardy turns from this painful subject back to the source of his consolation—the memory of their days of happiness. Emma's ghost has the authority and corporeality of the traditional-ballad ghost in Hardy's mind as she leads him 'To the spots we knew when we haunted here together'. The bewilderment of verse I is replaced by a new confidence in what is happening to him. The physical actuality of the places he revisits evokes memories that are so powerful that the past merges into the present, a process of reliving the past that finds its final triumphant consolation in the rediscovery of that love for Emma that had been soured by so many years of discord:

> Trust me, I mind not, though Life lours,
>   The bringing me here; nay, bring me here again!
>   I am just the same as when
> Our days were a joy, and our paths through flowers.

Hardy does not delude himself into believing that past events are being physically re-enacted or that Emma is an actual ghost that might be seen by birds or frighten seals. They are 'Ignorant of what there is flitting here to see' because it all takes place within the mind of Hardy—but it is no less real to Hardy for that.

NOTES AND GLOSSARY:

ejaculations: the sea makes sudden and awesome noises as it strikes against the cliff-face, surging in and out of unseen hollows in the rock

lours: seems threatening
In line 30 Gibson's *Chosen Poems of Thomas Hardy* misprints 'may' for
'nay'. The line should read 'nay, bring me here again!'. 'Nay' is an old
form of 'no'.

'Beeny Cliff'

Having securely rediscovered the past, Hardy wrote this poem as a vivid
re-enactment and celebration of that day in March 1870 when Emma
took him to see Beeny Cliff. The scene is described in a rich, dazzling,
brightly-coloured manner, 'opal and the sapphire' of the sea, Emma's
'bright hair', the 'clear-sunned March day'. Even the rain is 'irised', and
the momentary darkness only acts as a foil to the sun which 'bursts out
again, and purples prinked the main'. The richness of the diction is
joined with a luxurious use of alliteration, 'wandering western sea', 'we
laughed light-heartedly aloft' (containing also assonance—similar or
identical vowel sounds in proximity), and 'wild weird western shore'.
The long lines move with an easy rhythm, the triple rhymes binding each
stanza together. There is a sense of lightness, joy and freedom, Emma is
'riding high above', her 'bright hair flapping free'. But then verses IV and
V bring in Hardy's characteristic perspective, contrasting the relative
permanence of nature with the transitoriness of human life. The cliff is
still there 'in all its chasmal beauty' but Emma is 'elsewhere'. Only on
that word 'elsewhere' does the swinging rhythm meet a check. The end of
the poem is full of sadness for lost love, youth and joy, but it is a resigned
sadness and not an anguished one.

NOTES AND GLOSSARY:
mews: seagulls
plained: *(archaic, poetic)* the cry of seagulls is a plaintive,
complaining sound
nether: *(archaic)* lower
irised: coloured with a rainbow
prinked: decorated, bedecked
main: sea
chasmal: rock that is deeply fissured or cracked

'During Wind and Rain'

This superb elegy seems to have been influenced by Hardy reading
Emma's account of her childhood in Plymouth in her manuscript *Some
Recollections* which he discovered after her death. The personal
references are, however, not important because the poem's subject is of
universal significance and the character of the family involved is

deliberately generalised so that it represents families and human life in general. The poem is very skilfully constructed. The first five lines of each stanza describe a scene of liveliness, hope and family harmony. Notice that in each verse the family work or play together in agreement and their actions are always constructive, which is emphasised by the repetition of the affirmative 'aye' or 'yea'. Against these positive, life-affirming images are set the threatening images of the last two lines of each stanza, beginning with the emotional ballad-like refrain, 'Ah, no; the years O!' or 'Ah, no; the years, the years'. Although the positive scenes are given in the present tense, the refrain changes the perspective so that the scenes are seen to be in the past being viewed from an unhappier present, literally, as the final lines indicate, during wind and rain. The images of storm and autumn in these final lines also have a metaphorical significance by their association with death. This is made explicit in the final line of the poem, 'Down their carved names the rain-drop ploughs', which suggests that even the memorial of their carved names on the gravestones will be obliterated by natural forces in the course of time.

The poem is effective because of the way in which the contrasts between life and death are made. The images of life are given with such precise, pictorial detail that we are convinced of the beauty, loveliness and warm fellowship of life. Against this are relentlessly set the dark, threatening images that point to the transitory nature of this life. Both sets of images are given in the present tense, adding to their immediacy, but because of the time switch demanded by the refrain, the images of life are transferred into the past at the end of each verse. The reader is forced in each verse to experience the process of the present becoming the past, not in the familiar way of one day following another, but on the vaster time-scale of death following life. This awareness of man's mortality in the midst of his life is typical of Hardy's way of thinking, and 'During Wind and Rain' is one of his supreme expressions of the pathos of human joys when viewed from this perspective.

NOTES AND GLOSSARY:

one to play: one person to play the piano

'Channel Firing'

This poem was written in April 1914, four months before the outbreak of the First World War. It is narrated by one of the dead, probably in Stinsford churchyard, who is disturbed by the sound of the British Navy's gunnery practice in the English Channel. The poem is humorous in tone but serious in intent. Because of the noise the dead think it must be Judgement Day, but God casually informs them that it is only gunnery practice at sea. He condemns war and says that it is fortunate for the war-mongers that this is not Judgement Day because they would have 'to scour/Hell's floor' for their threatening behaviour. God grimly says it will be more awesome when Judgement Day comes, if indeed it ever does as man's condition is so wretched he is in need of eternal rest. One of the dead wonders if the world will become saner and renounce war, but 'many a skeleton shook his head'. Parson Thirdly regrets that his years of preaching against inhumanities have made such little impact, 'I wish I had stuck to pipes and beer'. The final verse drops the colloquial, grimly humorous tone and adopts a wider geographical and historical view. The three places mentioned represent powerful Wessex dynasties that have perished. The suggestion is that just as men will not learn to avoid war through the teachings of Christ, so they will not learn by bitter experience.

NOTES AND GLOSSARY:

chancel:	eastern part of a church where the altar stands
glebe cow:	clergyman's cow grazing on church land
mad as hatters:	people who made hats used to use a substance that affected their brains
blow the trumpet:	it is said that Judgement Day will be announced by the sound of trumpets
Stourton Tower:	a tower erected to commemorate the Anglo-Saxon King Alfred
Camelot:	the court of the Celtic King Arthur, said to be near Glastonbury
Stonehenge:	a stone circle erected by a British civilisation that preceded the Celts

---

'In Time of "The Breaking of Nations"'

This poem was written in 1915 during the First World War. The title is taken from the Bible, Jeremiah 51:20, 'Thou art my battle axe and weapons of war: for with thee will I break in pieces the nations, and with thee will I destroy kingdoms.' The poem expresses Hardy's conviction that the virtues of labour and love will outlive the power of great dynasties and the devastation of wars. The labourer and his old horse are 'half asleep' as they break up the clods of earth in the field in preparation for sowing. The 'couch-grass', a common weed, burns away without flame. These things seem insignificant and humble, yet they will continue and be needed by man for his bodily sustenance when dynasties have passed. The third verse raises the diction of the poem by using archaic words, 'Yonder', 'maid', 'wight', 'Ere'. The elevated diction marks the lovers as symbolic of all lovers and also suggests that love is timeless, the greatest of all men's qualities, and brighter and more passionate than the equally necessary but slow and toilsome business of earning one's daily bread.

NOTES AND GLOSSARY:
Yonder: *(archaic)* over there
maid: *(archaic)* young unmarried woman
wight: *(archaic)* man
Ere: *(archaic)* before

'Nobody Comes'

Hardy wrote 'Nobody Comes' on 9 October 1924 when his second wife was leaving the London nursing-home where she had undergone an operation. Probably the poem expresses Hardy's disappointed expectation of her arrival and his loneliness at Max Gate without her. The first verse sets the dreary scene with its emphasis on emptiness and darkness, 'the fainting light', 'the crawl of night', 'the darkening land', the ghostly noise of the telegraph wire to the town. This lonely scene is suddenly shattered by the noise and glare of a car, but 'It has nothing to do with me', and by contrast leaves 'a blacker air'. Hardy is left in the gloom, '... again alone/And nobody pulls up there'. This is a remarkably modern poem in its setting and its sense of the isolation of one person from another--the lonely watcher and the car which 'whangs along in a world of its own'.

NOTES AND GLOSSARY:
fainting light/... crawl of night: evening steadily turns into night
whangs: *(colloquial)* the sound of a car as it approaches and passes a bystander

---

'Afterwards'

This poem comes at the end of the volume *Moments of Vision*, published in 1917 when Hardy was seventy-seven. It is concerned with how he would like to be remembered after death, which he describes as Time closing a 'postern' behind his 'tremulous' time on earth. Each verse considers a different moment when he might die, and the actions of the creatures and sights of nature that would accompany his death at such a moment. The descriptions of nature, animal- and bird-life are vivid and detailed, and Hardy wishes to be remembered as 'a man who used to notice such things', and as one who 'strove that such innocent creatures should come to no harm'. Considering Hardy's fame and honours at this time of his life, there is a touching modesty in this prosaic wish. There is also an unusual spirit of peace and quietism in the poem. The natural scenes are observed with a typical love for their small details and a relish for their simple actuality, but there is no hint of Hardy's gloom, no ironical comment on the future fate of the 'glad green leaves' of May. Even the common Hardy images of death are described in positive terms—the night is 'mothy and warm', and winter is mysterious and lovely with its 'full-starred heavens'. Hardy does not wish to be remembered as the pessimist or the prophet crying in the wilderness but as the simple countryman with the caring, observing eye.

NOTES AND GLOSSARY:

latched:	fastened a door or gate
postern:	*(archaic)* small door or gate
tremulous:	frail or transitory
bell of quittance:	the bell that rings from a church at a funeral

---

'A Trampwoman's Tragedy'

Although not in normal ballad metre, this poem is certainly a ballad in its dramatic narrative form, its incidents and atmosphere. It was written in 1902, and Hardy said it is 'a ballad based on some local story of an event more or less resembling the incidents embodied, which took place between 1820 and 1830'. The story is told by the only survivor of the tragedy, the trampwoman. She had wandered over many areas of western England with three companions, her 'fancy-man', jeering John and Mother Lee. They were all tramps, outside the mainstream of settled society and dependent on each other for comradeship:

> For months we had padded side by side,
> Ay, side by side. . . .

On some 'deadly day' she began to tease her lover by pretending that she had transferred her affections to jeering John. It was an act of 'wanton idleness', irrational, inexplicable and threatening. When they arrived at 'Marshal's Elm' inn, she pretended that the baby she bore was John's and not her lover's. In a frenzy of jealousy, her lover murdered John. Revenge is a typical emotion and motive in ballads—it is the theme of Hardy's 'The Sacrilege'. Society took its revenge by hanging her lover for the murder. The trampwoman, alone because Mother Lee has also died, gave birth to 'his dead-born child'. Finally, her lover's ghost appeared and asked her once again whose child it was. She replied honestly that it was his, on which 'he smiled, and thinned away' leaving her alone and friendless, 'Haunting the Western Moor'.

It is a stark and powerful story of elemental passions set against a lonely background. There is a sense of fatality about the story, emphasised by the repetition in the second line of each verse which drums home significant actions or the trampwoman's emotional state:

Thereaft I walked the world alone,
  Alone, alone!

This is especially effective in stanza IX in suspending the dramatic action before the murder. Hardy regarded this as one of his most successful poems.

NOTES AND GLOSSARY:
Wynyard's Gap: fifteen miles north-west of Dorchester
fosseway: an ancient road
turnpike tracks: the turnpike was a gate set across a road in order to take a toll from the road-users
fancy-man: *(archaic)* lover
tap: inn
tor and lea: hill and meadow
settle: bench with a high back and arms
Gilded: coloured gold
ta'en: taken
Blue Jimmy: a notorious horse-thief
steed: horse
dropt: gave birth to

'A Sunday Morning Tragedy'

Written in 1904, this ballad is set in a remote region of Dorset in the 1860s. The narrator is mother to a beautiful girl who becomes a 'thrall', enslaved by love, to a man who makes her pregnant—'she had loved too well'. The mother pleads with the man but he refuses to marry the girl. In desperation the mother goes to a shepherd who gives her a herb intended to cause abortion, ' "'Tis meant to balk ill-motherings" '; but it kills the girl and she dies on the very Sunday that her lover comes to tell her that he intends to marry her after all.

This poem has the same stark, passionate intensity of 'A Tramp-woman's Tragedy', and it is achieved in a similar way. In both poems the narrator is the protagonist, and although the verse form is simpler in 'A Sunday Morning Tragedy' there is the same skilful use of refrain and repetition. The simple quatrain form is broken and weighted by the tolling refrain 'alas for me', or by key phrases such as 'wronged, sinless she', and 'the bride to be'. These act as a type of emotional comment and emphasis, keeping the narrator's sense of anguish constantly before the reader. They contrast with the dramatic action which is told in a bald, straightforward manner.

The dramatic irony found in this poem is typical of many of Hardy's poems. The attempt at abortion is unnecessary as the lover intended to marry her after all, and she died on the very day her banns were called and everyone crowds into her cottage to greet her. A further irony is that the events are only precipitated by her lover's flippant joke of keeping his intention to marry her a secret:

"'Twas done to please her, we surmise?'
(They spoke quite lightly in their glee)
'Done by him as a fond surprise?'
I thought their words would madden me.

Similarly in 'A Trampwoman's Tragedy' the deadly events are precipitated by mere 'teasing'.

The mother finally rejects the social morality that in the name of Christianity condemns illegitimacy, 'the plight/That is so scorned in Christendie', when she calls her daughter 'wronged, sinless she'. The mother feels that it is she herself who has sinned in transgressing the law of nature that her daughter had followed. In praying that God should *not* pity her she continues to reject the forgiving Christian God. Hardy implies that the social morality of his time is neither in keeping with natural laws nor with the true spirit of Christianity.

NOTES AND GLOSSARY:

shroud:	the sheet in which the dead are wrapped
traps:	personal belongings
main:	sea
Wessex:	an ancient name for western England which Hardy revived and popularised. It is the region that appears in his writing
beholds:	*(archaic)* sees
subtle:	clever
Christendie:	Christendom
curfew strook:	the bell struck at its fixed hour in the evening
white smock:	farm labourers used to wear a white outer garment like a long shirt
crook:	shepherds carry a hooked staff to assist them in their work
poppling:	the rolling and turning of boiling water
'Here's physic for untimely fruit':	here is a medicine for an unwanted pregnancy
betimes:	in good time
raiment:	*(archaic)* fine clothing
sackcloth-clad:	dressed in sackcloth, a coarse fabric that was worn when mourning for the dead

banns:	an announcement of the intention to marry, called three times on successive Sundays in church before the marriage ceremony (see line 107)
bantered:	. joked
wantonly:	cruelly, without purpose
pictotee:	a type of carnation, a flower

'Weathers'

This is an unusually cheerful poem that delights both by what it says and how it says it. The first verse describes the pleasant weather of spring or early summer; the second verse describes unpleasant weather, probably in late autumn. The poem is constructed on a scheme of parallels and contrasts. In verse I the rain falls in pleasant showers and there is a sense of growth, purpose and expansion into light and air after the confinement of winter. In verse II the rain is dreary and destructive, causing beeches to drip and meadow rivulets to overflow. There is a sense of nature and mankind seeking shelter before the hardships of winter:

And rooks in families homeward go,
    And so do I.

The formal contrasts and parallels are similarly marked. Notice that each line in verse II begins with the same word as in verse I. Notice also the rhyme scheme and the evocative use of rhythm. For instance, the four stresses of line 5 in verse I are distributed over eleven syllables. In contrast, the four stresses of the same line in verse II are distributed over only eight syllables. Contrary to what you might expect, the syllabically shorter line seems to take longer to read than the syllabically longer line. This is because the English language, unlike many languages, is timed by stress and not by the number of syllables. What happens, therefore, when you read a line with many syllables is that you rush over the syllables to reach the fixed, main stresses:

And the little brown nightingale bills his best.

The line has a lightness and a bouncy rhythm, reinforced by the alliterative 'b's', that is wholly appropriate. By contrast, the stressed words are more heavily weighted in the syllabically shorter line, giving an appropriate sense of the ponderous, powerful surge of the sea, reinforced by the alliterative 'th' sounds:

And hill-hid tides throb, throe on throe.

The impetus in English is to give lines with the same number of stresses identical timing; the effect is to spend longer on the stresses in syllabically shorter lines, and to bounce off the stresses more quickly in syllabically longer lines in order not to spend more time reading or saying the many syllables.

The pervading sense of delight throughout this poem is partly due to the repetition of 'And so do I' in both verses. For once, Hardy is absolutely in harmony with nature and his fellow men, whether they are sitting outside at the inn or shunning foul weather. If the weather is bad, he too, like the rooks, can hasten homeward with its suggestions of shelter, comfort and warmth.

NOTES AND GLOSSARY:

nestlings: the young birds born in spring and early summer
bills: sings
sprig-muslin drest: wearing light cotton dresses
dream of the south and west: perhaps because these are the warmest parts of England where people go for their holidays
duns: dull greyish-brown colours
thresh, and ply: thrash and bend in the wind
hill-hid tides: the sea hidden behind the hill
rivulets: small rivers or streams

'An August Midnight'

This poem, written at Max Gate in 1899, illustrates a characteristic of Hardy's poetry very well. The poem appears simple, almost banal, and it makes no profound claim to significance or special poetic insight; yet the effect of its microscopic focus on life and its wonder and respect for the humblest life, conveys a moving sense of a man compassionately searching for meaning in a baffling world. It does so with a gentle sense of humour; as J. O. Bailey remarked, 'The reflections have his peculiar blend of humour, compassion and philosophic thought.'* It is difficult to imagine another poet who could have made such a delightful poem out of the inconsequential meeting of the poet and some insects that blunder on to his page at night. To begin with there is the characteristic setting of the scene by describing selected parts of it; literally a 'scene', a small drama of life in which the verbs are prominent, describing the typical actions of blind, clock and insects. The second verse ponders the significance of what is happening. Hardy's awareness of the fellowship of all life can be seen by the way he counts himself with the insects, 'Thus meet we five'. The insects' actions appear meaningless and ridiculous:

—My guests besmear my new-penned line,
Or bang at the lamp and fall supine.

*In *The Poetry of Thomas Hardy*, University of North Carolina Press, Chapel Hill, 1970, p.162.

The rhyme is intentionally humorous. Their actions prompt Hardy to ponder on their humble state, and yet 'They know Earth-secrets that know not I'. This is not claiming that they know some profound secret hidden from the poet, but that we should respect the fact that other creatures have their place in the order of things and, however humble, are able to perceive aspects of life of which we are unaware.

NOTES AND GLOSSARY:

longlegs:	a type of fly with very long legs
dumbledore:	either a large bee or a flying beetle, a cockchafer
supine:	on their backs

'Snow in the Suburbs'

In this poem Hardy seems delighted by the sheer act of describing what he sees, and he feels under no compulsion to justify the description by making any comment or ascribing any particular value to it. It is true that the final line where the Hardys take in a stray cat shows human compassion to animals, but it is stated in the same matter-of-fact manner as the rest of the poem. Hardy wrote several such poems, especially late in his life, delighting in description for its own sake and the playful use of diction, rhyme and rhythm. Notice, for instance, that the main stresses in the last line of verse I fall in a patterned manner on the alliterative words 'waft of wind' and 'fleecy fall'. The line seems to dance like the falling snowflakes. Compare this with the last line of verse II which is appropriately congested, to such an extent that it is difficult to know how to scan it. The sparrow in the second verse is unintentionally comic, and this is reflected in the playful internal rhyme of:

> And overturns him,
> And near inurns him. . . .

But the onlookers are not cruel, as the final quatrain testifies.

NOTES AND GLOSSARY:

palings:	a fence made out of pointed pieces of wood bound together with a small space between each piece
fleecy:	literally a fleece is the wool of a sheep; the image is of the falling of light, white snowflakes
inurns:	entombs, buries
blanched:	whitened

'Ah, Are You Digging on My Grave?'

This poem is constructed on the question and answer pattern found in traditional ballads such as 'Edward' and in many folk-songs. A dead woman inquires who is digging on her grave and the succession of answers comes as a series of disillusionments. It is neither her husband, who has just married someone else, nor her relatives, nor her enemy, but her dog. She praises the faithfulness of the dog which seems to outlive that of humans, but the dog's final comment comes as a surprising and ultimate disillusionment. Even the dog has forgotten its mistress and merely uses her grave as a convenient place to bury a bone. The poem is making a serious point about how quickly the dead can be forgotten, but it should not be taken too seriously as the tone is wryly humorous, underlined by the frivolous triple rhyme, 'spot/ trot/ forgot'.

The irony in this poem is typical of Hardy's view of life— that what is expected is good but what actually happens is sad. Sometimes, though, the opposite can occur. Hardy expresses his faith in 'evolutionary meliorism' when 'loving-kindness' replaces the negative feelings of revenge and jealousy in such poems as 'The Burghers' and 'A Wife and Another'. Although Hardy's outlook on life is usually tragic, one should not expect complete consistency of attitude from one poem to the next. 'Ah, Are You Digging on My Grave?' is, for instance, quite different from 'Friends Beyond' where Hardy pictures the dead as happily at rest and careless of the things they most prized in life and even of the memory of the living.

NOTES AND GLOSSARY:

rue: an evergreen shrub associated with sad remembrance

tendance: tending, care

gin: trap

Part 3

Commentary

THE NOTES SO FAR should have helped you to understand the meaning of the poems better and towards a deeper and fuller response to them. The purpose of this part is to analyse the poetry so that we can understand why we respond to it in the way we do. In other words, we must understand not only what Hardy is saying but how he is saying it, his poetic method. There are many clues to his method scattered around in the previous part because each poem studied in detail tends to raise certain points about method and its interrelatedness with theme. This section intends to bring these scattered comments together, to synthesise them, so that we can understand Hardy's achievement as a whole.

Irony

Hardy's form of irony is usually dramatic irony in which the actions of people or of fate are contrary to what is expected or hoped for. In 'Convergence of the Twain', for example, man labours to build the mighty, unsinkable ship while the 'Immanent Will' quietly creates the iceberg that will sink it. This is irony on a cosmic level, raising moral questions about the nature of the universe, whether it is controlled by a good, a malignant or an indifferent force. These questions are often behind Hardy's poems though usually they are asked less clearly, being implied through irony on an individual level, as in 'Ah, Are You Digging on My Grave?' where the dead woman's expectations are systematically negated. Some might say that the irony here is too systematic, too obviously contrived by Hardy rather than arising naturally from the situation. After all, it is not necessarily a sign of disrespect for the dead wife when the husband remarries—life must go on. Hardy is sometimes guilty of forcing irony in this way, both in his poems and his novels, and then we feel that his pessimistic inclinations have led him to distort truth. But the irony in this particular poem is of a grimly humorous nature that does not invite us to take its point too seriously about the value of life that can be so easily forgotten. It is an instance of Hardy's grim rustic humour, a tone in his poetry that sophisticated, urban critics have often failed to recognise, with the result that a poem can be taken too earnestly at its face value as an example of Hardy's 'pessimism'. This sense of humour went with a side to Hardy's personality that did seem rather to enjoy being gloomy. His second wife, Florence, wrote in a letter, 'T.H.

... is now, this afternoon, writing a poem with great spirit: always a sign of well-being with him. Needless to say, it is an intensely dismal poem.'

Usually, however, Hardy does intend his ironical view of life to be taken very seriously indeed. In 'A Trampwoman's Tragedy' the irony is both individual and serious, and lies in the fact that the murder and all that stems from it was a ghastly accident as the woman was never unfaithful to her lover. Similarly, in 'A Sunday Morning Tragedy' there was no need for the mother to give her daughter the drug that tragically killed her because the daughter's lover intended to marry her. This irony is harrowing because we experience the individual suffering that arises from it; at the same time it poses broad moral questions about the nature of the universe we inhabit where such things can take place. It is, however, possible on this level both to sympathise with the individual's suffering and to accuse him or her of causing it. The trampwoman should never have teased her lover; the mother should never have risked her daughter's life in an attempt to avoid the social scandal of illegitimacy. The fault, we might argue, is not in the nature of the universe but in the nature of the individual.

It is at the level of Hardy's more lyrical, often personal poems that we find his ironical view of life working at its subtlest and its most effective. 'The Self-Unseeing' is ironical in its view that we only really appreciate happiness when it is in the past and we look back at it from a less happy present. We do not feel this is a personal failing of Hardy but an expression of a universal truth; nostalgia is a typical Hardy mood but it is not the sentimental nostalgia for 'the good old days' that never existed, rather it is the expression of man's mortality, an awareness of the inevitable passing away of things. The 'Poems of 1912–13' work on this level. Although they are concerned with intensely personal events in Hardy's life, their ironical perspective draws general truths from the particular situations. For instance, 'At Castle Boterel' celebrates the ability of the memory to keep alive the joys of the past while at the same time acknowledging that the memories and the joys must die with the individual. This is the explicit subject of several poems where a dead lover is seen as having only a limited 'immortality' in the memory of his or her surviving partner (see, for instance, 'Her Immortality'). This is the view of a man whose life spans many years, an essentially ironical perspective of man's joys that gives rise to compassion and pathos in Hardy rather than to cynicism or despair. It was this lofty, bird's-eye view of life that W. H. Auden (1907–73) so admired in Hardy and emulated in his own poetry.*

'During Wind and Rain' is a particularly clear example of the Hardy

---

* Auden was one of the most distinguished twentieth-century poets; for his comments on Hardy see 'A Literary Transference' in A. J. Guerard (ed.), *Hardy* (Twentieth Century Views), Prentice-Hall, New Jersey, 1963, pp.135–142.

perspective. Again he is viewing with compassion past scenes of happiness from a sad present, but the fact of decay and death in the present does not negate past joys in the sense of making them worthless. On the contrary, past joys seem even more precious and lovely because of their contrast with present sadness—the mood that underlines 'The Self-Unseeing'. Hardy is never against life's joys; it is an error on the part of the believers in 'The Impercipient' to charge Hardy 'that blessed things/ I'd liefer not have be'. It is Hardy's temperament, his rigorous honesty that compels him always to take 'a full look at the Worst', to acknowledge man's mortality and the transitoriness of his joys. Middleton Murry (1889–1957) commented on Hardy, 'The great poet remembers both rose and thorn; and it is beyond his powers to remember them otherwise than as together.'* The impression of Hardy's poems at their best is that he is always in possession of the relentless, piteous truth, as any profound ironist must be.

However, many readers and many other poets would regard Hardy's truth as only partial. All the world's religions offer their believers hope that death is not the end but the beginning of a new and potentially more joyful life. As we have seen in 'The Impercipient', Hardy had lost his religious belief and with it he had lost hope in a future life. A religious apprehension of rebirth may be in the 'blessed Hope' of which the bird sings in 'A Darkling Thrush' at the beginning of the new century, but Hardy has to admit humbly that it is a hope of which he is 'unaware'. He is restricted by the scientific materialism of the age which subjects religion to rational inquiry and finds it wanting. Hardy speaks powerfully to the twentieth century because he was one of the first and most unswerving poets to confront this question. He regarded himself as a monist and tried to write monistic poetry. A monist is someone who holds that all life, all matter is fundamentally of one nature. Belief in a world of spirits, of God and the devil, alongside the world of man and nature, is a form of dualism, an acceptance of two wholly different levels of existence that cannot be proved and is therefore irrational. Monism is a limiting factor for a poet because, as Hardy realised, poetry is essentially concerned with man's 'spirit', with the irrational, religious side of man's nature. For instance, poetry tends to project human feelings and consciousness on to inanimate nature, an irrational tendency that Hardy recognised in himself, 'In spite of myself I cannot help noticing countenances and tempers in objects of scenery, e.g. trees, hills, houses' (*The Life*, p.285).

There is strength as well as limitation in this view of the world and of poetry. Hardy cannot permit himself either the personal ecstacy of the

*Murry was a distinguished editor and critic; for his essay on Hardy see J. Gibson and T. Johnson (eds.), *Thomas Hardy: Poems* (Casebook Series), Macmillan, London, 1979, pp.81–91.

Romantic poet or the conscious retreat to received religion of some Victorian poets. He is confronted by and confronts the facts of naked mortality, and can find consolation only in the 'moments of vision' of his poetry. This 'vision' is rigorously monistic; it is 'earth-bound', and consists in the re-creation through memory in his poetry of moments of great earthly joy as an unreflecting child or lover. Hence the importance of memory to Hardy and the complex nature of his ghosts. Ghosts, such as Emma in the 'Poems of 1912–13', have no existence in a dualistic sense, but are very real in a monistic sense in that they exist within the mind of the person who is remembering. Thus they are a potent force in defying time and preserving those memories which give value to life. The ultimate tragedy is that the memories die with the individual, and within the poetry it is part of Hardy's particular vision always to acknowledge this truth in order to avoid delusion. A stoical, steadfast acceptance of man's mortality and life's sadness is an essential part of Hardy's vision, of one who, as he wrote in 'In Tenebris I', 'Waits in unhope'. Hardy suggests that value and meaning in life have to be continually re-created by each individual within a world that has no inherent value, except perhaps the slow development of man's sense of 'loving-kindness'.

We have seen what Hardy values—those earthly moments of joy, the memory of them and the re-creation of them in poetry, the slow evolution of 'loving-kindness' and the stoical acceptance of man's mortality. Against this is set an indifferent universe without inherent meaning beyond its own mechanical continuance. The question Hardy faced was how to write poetry affirming his humble but infinitely precious values in this meaningless world. In the midst of the horrors of the First World War, Hardy wrote a poem called 'I Looked Up from My Writing' where the all-seeing moon challenges the value of his poetic endeavours:

> 'And now I am curious to look
>   Into the blinkered mind
> Of one who wants to write a book
>   In a world of such a kind.'

The chilling implication is that all endeavour is pointless in a brutal world, a view that brings us to contemporary absurdist literature. Yet Hardy had positive values and published over nine hundred poems, and these poems represent an exploration of and statement of the values that he hammered out from the threateningly meaningless flow of experience.

The main principle that Hardy adopted to achieve this ordering of life's experiences was the pattern suggested to him by his ironical perspective. A. S. MacDowall (1876–1933)* recognised this when he

* MacDowall was a critic and leader-writer for *The Times*; for his essays see *Thomas Hardy: Poems*, pp.111–29.

wrote that Hardy's irony 'weaves the chaos of things into a pattern'. Irony brings structure to life and to Hardy's poetry because it is able to bring together apparently separate areas of experience and to suggest that they are significant. Thus, in 'Convergence of the Twain' the fatal conjunction of ship and iceberg is not a wholly meaningless accident but shows a significant plan, apparently related to humbling man's pride, but ultimately a mystery with sinister overtones. Similarly, Hardy cannot be sure there is hope in the bird's song in 'A Darkling Thrush', but it carries significance because of its ironic contrast with the desolate surroundings and his own sense of hopelessness:

> So little cause for carolings
>   Of such ecstatic sound
> Was written on terrestial things
>   Afar or nigh around,
> That I could think there trembled through
>   His happy good-night air
> Some blessed Hope, whereof he knew
>   And I was unaware.

Hardy's ironical perspective is most clearly seen in a poem such as 'During Wind and Rain' where the images of life are systematically juxtaposed with images of death. It is less obvious in the 'Poems of 1912–13' but it nevertheless exists on two levels, between poems and within poems. As a series, a poem of doubt is often answered by a poem of affirmation, and this is part of Hardy's typical contrasting pattern of light against dark, past against present, happiness against sorrow, affirmation against despair. Thus, the question in 'The Haunter':

> He does not think that I haunt here nightly:
>   How shall I let him know

is partly answered by 'The Voice'. The question in 'A Dream or No': 'Why go to Saint Juliot? What's Juliot to me?' is triumphantly answered by 'After a Journey': 'Hereto I come to view a voiceless ghost'. 'Beeny Cliff' celebrates Hardy's memories but ends with the question:

> What if still in chasmal beauty looms that wild weird western shore,
> The woman now is—elsewhere—whom the ambling pony bore,
> And nor knows nor cares for Beeny, and will laugh there
>   nevermore.

This is answered in 'At Castle Boterel' where, for the remembering man, the places evoke and come to symbolise the joy of love.

It may be noticed from this pattern that the more intense and richer poems are those of affirmation rather than those of questioning or despair (apart from 'The Going' which stands alone in having the germ of the whole pattern within it). The reason for this is that the ironic contrasts are more at work in the affirmative poems. 'The Haunter' is written from Emma's point of view as a ghost in the present and lacks sufficiently the past versus present perspective, though the second verse where there is this perspective is significantly the most poignant. 'A Dream or No' dwells almost totally in the past and doubts the truth of its existence as a present reality, thus abandoning the tension that Hardy achieves through the interaction of past with present. 'Beeny Cliff' similarly lacks this enriching tension, living almost entirely, albeit vividly, in the past and doubting its relevance to the present. However, 'The Voice', 'After a Journey' and 'At Castle Boterel' engage directly in the problems of relating past memories to present experience and achieve that vital interaction between past and present on which the success of so many of Hardy's finest poems is built.

Although the irony of circumstances seems to suggest significance in life, the nature of the significance often remains mysterious. Hardy was an earnest student of philosophy, hoping to discover a meaning in life that he had lost with his faith, but his conclusion was that:

> Unadjusted impressions have their value, and the road to a true philosophy of life seems to lie in humbly recording diverse readings of its phenomena as they are forced upon us by chance and change.
>   (preface to *Poems of the Past and the Present*).

Hence his avid interest in all kinds of stories, from the most outlandish to the most apparently trivial—one could never tell where a vital truth might be lurking. So, as we have seen, he was content at times to describe a scene without giving it any particular significance, as in 'Snow in the Suburbs'. Or he became engrossed in the apparently trivial, as in the conjunction of the poet and four insects in 'An August Midnight', leading him to ponder on its possible significance:

> Thus meet we five, in this still place,
> At this point of time, at this point in space.
> —My guests besmear my new-penned line,
> Or bang at the lamp and fall supine.
> 'God's humblest, they!' I muse. Yet why?
> They know Earth-secrets that know not I.

Notice the characteristic focus on 'this still place', 'this point of time', 'this point in space'—for all its apparent triviality, the apparently meaningless activity of the insects, and in spite of their inability to reveal their 'Earth-secrets', this is a tiny 'moment of vision', a feeling of fellowship with other creatures, the poet's 'guests'. Of course, this is not simply a matter of 'humbly recording' life, because the poet's impressions, however 'unadjusted' must give some value to that life. But, as the poet C. Day Lewis (1904–72) said, '... Hardy will not force his feelings beyond the limit which his reason has fixed, will not let himself be carried away by pity, to make the poem more hopeful or more "poetical".'* Hardy's verse is always austerely sincere. The sense of anguish and remorse in 'The Going' or the pity for man's mortality that pervades 'During Wind and Rain' is not alleviated either by false hopes or the extraneous beauty of musical verse. Hardy resolutely views the ironies of life and records them with a compassion that is all the consolation he has to offer.

Narrative

Hardy was brought up in the traditional, oral culture of pre-industrial England. He attended harvest suppers where ancient ballads and folk-songs were still sung, and he was an accomplished folk-violinist, playing folk-tunes and dances at local Dorset parties. He began making a collection of traditional Dorset verse as early as the 1870s before there was much interest in the surviving evidence of the oral tradition as a living culture. The ballad view of life and approach to poetry was his own by birthright, and the influence is clear in both his prose and verse. 'A Trampwoman's Tragedy' is close to the traditional ballad world which was a dark, violent one ruled by passion and a retributive code of justice. There were few values beyond earthly loyalty and love. Religion played virtually no part as a softening influence in this harsh world of elemental passions and minimal order. The ballad stories, often superstitious and strange, are told as dramatic narratives with clear story-lines in which people reveal their natures by what they do or say. Even the expression of emotion is conveyed in terms of narrative action, except for the lyrical refrains in some ballads. If we take one of the most lyrical expressions of a state of mind in the traditional ballad, the lament in 'Mary Hamilton' before she is hanged, we find it is expressed in terms of past actions and their ironic contrast with present sorrow and her immediate fate:

Oh often have I dressed my queen
　An' put gold in her hair;
The gallows-tree is my reward
　An' shame must be my share.

Oh often have I dressed my queen
　An' soft, soft made her bed;
An' now I've got for my reward
　The gallows tree to tread.

* 'The Lyrical Poetry' in *Thomas Hardy: Poems*, p.148.

Oh little did my mother ken,
   That day she cradled me,
What lands I was to tread in
   Or what death I should dee.*

Hardy's poetic method is strikingly similar. In his lyrical poems, such as 'During Wind and Rain' or the 'Poems of 1912–13', the emotion arises out of vividly recalled and re-enacted *events* that contrast with the present sitaution. The lyricism, as in the traditional ballad, is expressed through dramatic narrative:

They clear the creeping moss—
Elders and juniors—aye,
Making the pathways neat
   And the garden gay;
And they build a shady seat. ...
   Ah, no; the years, the years;
See, the white storm-birds wing across!

This verse from 'During Wind and Rain' is entirely dramatic narrative except for the lyrical refrain 'Ah, no; the years, the years' which, as in the traditional ballad, directs our emotional response. Yet, although mainly dramatic, the poem is lyrical in its effect because the actions are generalised and designed to create images that contrast in an emotive fashion. Even Hardy's purest lyrics have their foundation in the narrative form. 'When I Set Out for Lyonnesse' is basically an account describing the journey there, what happened there, and what happened when the poet returned. 'Weathers' is about as far from the narrative as Hardy gets, except in philosophical poems such as 'The Impercipient' or 'And There Was a Great Calm'. Even in such poems, actions play an important part. The poet likes weather:

When showers betumble the chestnut spikes,
   And nestlings fly ...

He dislikes weather:

When beeches drip in browns and duns,
   And thresh and ply ...

and so on. If we add the many narrative ballads that Hardy wrote, such as 'A Trampwoman's Tragedy' and 'A Sunday Morning Tragedy', to the lyrics that depend on the dramatic form, we can understand why the poet Thom Gunn (b.1929) said of Hardy, 'The single important

*The text is taken from James Kinsley (ed.), *The Oxford Book of Ballads*, Oxford University Press, 1969, pp.330–1; the spelling has been modernised. 'Ken'=know; 'dee'=die. This sixteenth-century story is a mixture of incidents based on a queen's maid who was hanged for killing her illegitimate baby.

influence on him is that of the Ballads, and the majority of his poems derive either directly or indirectly from them.'*

The impersonality of the dramatic narrative was valuable to Hardy. It may seem strange to talk of the impersonality of Hardy's verse when the particular personality of the poet can be sensed behind every poem he wrote; but, even when biography tells us that a poem is personal, the dramatic narrative structure distances the poet from his creation. Direct personal expressions of emotion, like the cry of anguish at the end of 'The Going', are very rare in Hardy's poetry. He insisted on the impersonal nature of his verse in the prefaces to his first three books of poetry. In the preface to *Time's Laughingstocks* (1909) he wrote, '... the sense of disconnection (between poems), particularly in respect of those lyrics penned in the first person, will be immaterial when it is borne in mind that they are to be regarded, in the main, as dramatic monologues by different characters.' This statement is obviously designed as a shelter for his reticent nature, but the dramatic narrative did permit him to recount differing events, ideas and emotions without demanding that they be directly personal statements or placed within any clearly defined system of beliefs. Just as the irony brings together differing aspects of life without precisely defining their significance, so the dramatic narrative gave Hardy the liberty to tell a tale and let it speak for itself. Irony and narrative naturally go together in Hardy's poetry because both are dramatic and both are capable of implying rather than stating significance, as in the final verse of 'During Wind and Rain':

> They change to a high new house,
> He, she, all of them—aye,
> Clocks and carpets and chairs
>   On the lawn all day,
> And brightest things that are theirs. ...
>   Ah, no; the years, the years;
> Down their carved names the rain-drop ploughs.

Style

Irony is one of the major devices in Hardy's poetry, and his main poetic form is the dramatic narrative, even in most of those poems that are lyrical in effect. We shall now look more closely at his style.

Diction

In discussing Hardy's style, the distinguished critic F.R. Leavis (1895–1978) focused on its idiosyncratic nature when he said Hardy

*'The Influence of Ballad Forms' in *Thomas Hardy: Poems*, p.219.

makes a 'style out of stylelessness'.* In other words, Hardy does not take a received style and build on it, but forges a new style to express his personal vision. Much of the idiosyncrasy of this style lies in his use of diction. The style of Tennyson and Swinburne that he might have inherited was a particularly mellifluous one, striving for a musical beauty of sound that was often regarded as the essence of the 'poetical'. Hardy rejected this, saying, 'For as long as I can remember my instinctive feeling has been to avoid the jewelled line in poetry as being effeminate.' This is not to say that he was unable or unwilling to write a 'jewelled' line when it was appropriate, as in 'Beeny Cliff': 'O the opal and the sapphire of that wandering western sea'. Here he wishes to evoke a rich, romantic vision and so he opens the poem with the conventional lyric exclamation 'O', and quite literally resorts to jewels, 'the opal and the sapphire'. The alliteration of the 'w' and the 's' in 'wandering western sea' is the type of word music that the Victorians conventionally regarded as 'poetic'.

This type of line is very exceptional in Hardy's poetry. When he was writing an essay on the poet William Barnes, he said he admired Barnes's 'closeness of phrase to his vision', and this is something Hardy strove for in his own poetry.† As his vision of life was a sombre one, we would expect his poetry to reflect this by avoiding the 'jewelled line' and giving us something far less lulling, like this line from 'Wessex Heights': 'But mind chains do not clank where one's next neighbour is the sky'. Here a series of plosive sounds, /b, d, t, k/, evoke the clanking of chains which is an appropriate metaphor for the poet's agonised thoughts. The deliberately rugged quality of such lines has led to accusations of clumsiness and ugliness in his choice of words and of what Leavis called the 'gauche unshrinking mismarriages—group mismarriages—of his diction' ('Hardy the Poet', p.88). Certainly there is sometimes a gnarled quality about his diction that appears odd and difficult to read, as in this line from 'A Sign-Seeker', 'But that I fain would wot of shuns my sense'. This is from an early philosophical poem where his oddest diction is to be found, and it can be defended to a certain extent by saying that it reflects Hardy's struggle to use the English language to express the philosophical dilemmas of his day. In his maturer poems, however, Hardy was able to refer to philosophical ideas, using his customary terms, in such a way that the abstractions do not jar with the predominately conversational tone of a poem, as in this verse from 'At Castle Boterel':

And to me, though Time's unflinching rigour,
    In mindless rote, has ruled from sight

---

* In 'Hardy the Poet', *The Southern Review*, Louisiana State University Press, Louisiana, 1940, p.88.
† See Harold Orel, *Thomas Hardy's Personal Writing*, p.80.

The substance now, one phantom figure
   Remains on the slope, as when that night
     Saw us alight.

Hardy's diction is generally far more normal and conversational than has often been recognised. This is certainly true of the poems studied in detail in Part 2, and it can be argued that there is nothing clumsy or 'gauche' about his strange choice of words and contrasting levels of diction when they do appear. Hardy was a highly self-conscious artist and when he creates a 'mismarriage' of diction it is for a deliberate effect. We have seen that the first two verses of 'In Time of "The Breaking of Nations"' are wholly colloquial in their diction, except perhaps the capitalised 'Dynasties' which is designed to contrast with the rest of the poem. The third verse introduces vocabulary that is archaic and self-consciously 'poetic'—'maid', 'wight', 'Yonder', 'Ere'. The lovers are explicitly contrasted with 'War's annals', and on the level of diction they also contrast with the man 'harrowing clods', the 'old horse' and the 'couch-grass'. Conversational English describing a very ordinary scene is contrasted with an elevated diction describing the lovers, and the effect is to give the lovers a romantic aura, a higher status than the scenes of farm labour. By this economical stroke, Hardy suggests not only that love and labour will outlive dynasties and war, but that labour is a common, monotonous activity whereas love is man's opportunity for something higher.

Another striking example of Hardy's effective use of different levels of diction is found in 'And There Was a Great Calm', written to commemorate the end of the First World War. This begins on the level of philosophical abstractions, 'Passion', 'Despair', the 'Spirit of Pity', and so on. It moves to the ugly, prosaic words of war, 'dug-out', 'snipers', 'Huns'; and to the colloquial, '"Strange, this! How? All firing stopped?"'. In the final verse it returns to the abstractions. The effect of this is greatly to extend the range of questions that the poem asks about war and thus to extend our response. We view war not only from the lofty heights of philosophical speculation but from the viewpoint of the common man involved in it, of 'the bereft, and meek, and lowly', of the front-line soldier, and even of the uncomprehending animals. Questions are directly posed at each level; the only answer given is the fatalistic one of the 'Sinister Spirit', 'It had to be', the unsatisfactoriness of which is evident in the 'Spirit of Pity's' final, repeated question, 'Why?'.

There is no sense of poetic decorum in Hardy's verse, no acceptance of that consensus of opinion between poet and reader about what subjects and what words are suitable for poetry. For Hardy, all subjects and all words are equally suitable, and this is an essentially twentieth-century view. In all his poetry, and explicitly so in a poem such as 'And There

Was a Great Calm', there is a search for meaning in what appears to be a dark and meaningless world. As there is no consensus of opinion about the meaning of life, so there can be no received poetic decorum for the poet to follow. The poet's material becomes the whole of the language and he extracts what he needs from all levels of diction, including modern words—Hardy was one of the first to write of telegraph wires and cars with 'lamps full-glare' in 'Nobody Comes'. The range of Hardy's diction and its deliberate clashing of levels reflects the language of lost order seeking for meaning.

Imagery

Hardy is very restrained in his use of metaphor because metaphor assumes that there is an illuminating interrelatedness between things that are apparently dissimilar, that Hardy, from his monistic standpoint, can never be certain of. Frequently metaphor involves relating inanimate objects with the animate, as in the final lines of Wordsworth's (1770–1850) sonnet 'Composed Upon Westminster Bridge':

> Dear God! the very houses seem asleep;
> And all that mighty heart is lying still.

Here the inanimate houses and all the animate and inanimate objects that compose London are viewed as though they are a human-being with a heart who is asleep. It is difficult to imagine poetry that totally avoids making such relations, but Hardy is unwilling to make them with confidence. He tends to prefer simile to metaphor because simile states that one thing is like another rather than that one thing is another; the two elements remain discrete rather than being merged. For instance, from 'The Darkling Thrush':

> The tangled bine-stems scored the sky
> Like strings of broken lyres . . .

When he does use metaphor he often qualifies it with 'seem' or 'seemed':

> The land's sharp features seemed to be
> The Century's corpse outleant . . .

That is to say, it 'seemed' so to the poet but perhaps, as the thrush suggests, he is wrong. This restrained use of imagery has much to do with the characteristic mood in Hardy's poetry of a tentative and sincere movement towards meaning in a baffling universe.

Yet there is far more imagery in Hardy's verse than at first appears and it is, as T.R.M. Creighton writes,* '. . . embedded in Hardy's words and the way he uses them, not as a decoration but a function of

* In *Poems of Thomas Hardy*, Macmillan, London, 1979, p.xii.

language'. This imagery is often verbal: 'The *weakening* eye of day', 'The tangled bine-stems *scored* the sky', 'The Century's corpse *outleant*' (present writer's italics). Similarly, in 'During Wind and Rain' the emphasis is on the verbs, on the contrast between creative activity and destructive activity. Singing is contrasted with leaves that 'reel down in throngs'; clearing moss, making pathways neat and building a 'shady seat' is contrasted with storm-birds that 'wing across'; breakfasting is contrasted with 'the rotten rose ript from the wall'; changing to a new house is contrasted with the rain-drop that 'ploughs' down their carved names, preparing for a harvest of oblivion. The verbs often describe literal activities but they also carry metaphorical significance in that they represent the processes either of life or of death. The verbal activity evokes the sense of a family living happily through past time towards present death.

Because of Hardy's concern with actions through time and the recording of them as events in the dramatic narrative form, it is not surprising to find that many of his striking descriptions and images are verbal: 'I kissed her *colding* face and hair' ('A Sunday Morning Tragedy'); '... while I/ Saw morning *harden* upon the wall' ('The Going'); and from 'Lying Awake' where the poet imagines dawn breaking on familiar scenes:

> You, Churchyard, are lightening faint from the shade of the yew,
>   The names *creeping* out everywhere.

(Present writer's italics.)

'Colding' is a word coined by Hardy, a neologism, and there are some two hundred such words in the *Complete Poems*. It is not surprising to find that half of them are verbals: 'aftergrinds', 'downstairward', 'self-widowed', 'unadieued', 'unhope'. These reflect Hardy's attempt to achieve a 'closeness of phrase to his vision' of the dark side of life. The same impulse can be found in the many compound words he constructed, such as 'blast-beruffled', 'heart-halt' 'languid-lipped'. These compounds are frequently alliterative.

Syntax

Hardy has been accused of writing with unnecessarily contorted syntax, but unconventional word order is the exception rather than the rule. The first sentence of 'The Darkling Thrush' is typical, following the simple subject-verb-complement structure, the basic syntactical structure of the English language:

> I leant upon a coppice gate
>   When Frost was spectre-grey,

And Winter's dregs made desolate
  The weakening eye of day.

When Hardy deviates from this syntactical norm it invariably serves a
purpose. One such purpose has been called by T.R.M. Creighton
Hardy's 'grammar of grief'.* We have noticed that the complexity of the
grammar of verse I of 'The Voice' and verse II of 'After a Journey'
expresses the pain Hardy feels when writing about his past with Emma.
More specifically, the complexity of verse I of 'The Voice' reflects
Hardy's reluctance to touch on a painful subject of the past which might
impute blame to Emma. The long, winding sentence expresses reluctance
to refer to her changed nature and a desire to turn the sentence into an
affirmation of when 'our day was fair'. Verse II of 'After a Journey'
avoids any hint of blaming either party for the unhappiness and
attempts to summarise those painful years by presenting a series of short
questions as potential statements that Emma might make about those
years. The statements are tentatively offered, as though for Emma's
choosing, as a kind of peace-offering that concludes in the quiet
resignation of 'But all's closed now, despite Time's derision'. It will be
noticed that in the more self-confident, affirmative verses of these two
poems, the sentence may be long but there is less difficulty in
comprehension because the syntax is more conventional. Another poem
employing Hardy's 'grammar of grief' is 'A Broken Appointment' where
the delayed main clause 'Grieved I' creates a very complex sentence that
effectively takes the emphasis away from Hardy's personal grief and
places it on a statement about unselfish compassion. Verse II, where
Hardy's personal grief is under control and he is writing about the
incident with confidence in its message of general significance, has more
conventional syntax and is easily followed by the reader.

  Hardy is also very skilled in conveying conversation with all its
hesitations, false starts, repetitions and 'incomplete' grammar.
Although only one person is speaking in this verse from 'Julie-Jane', you
can sense the dialogue between speaker and poet in the pauses:

  —Tolling for her, as you guess;
    And the baby too. .... 'Tis well.
  You knew her in maidhood likewise?—Yes,
    That's her burial bell.

The third verse of 'The Man He Killed' exactly conveys the soldier's
hesitant, over-emphatic attempt to rationalise the inhumanity of war.
The last line of the verse is not end-stopped but pushes on into the next
verse as though the soldier is reaching out for the firmer ground of
shared humanity:

*In *Poems of Thomas Hardy*, p.vii.

'I shot him dead because—
Because he was my foe,
Just so: my foe of course he was;
That's clear enough; although

'He thought he'd 'list, perhaps,
Off-hand like—just as I—
Was out of work—had sold his traps—
No other reason why.'

Rhythm

The main controlling factor of rhythm in verse is metre, and Hardy was very interested in its technical aspects. Unlike T.S. Eliot (1888–1965) and Gerard Manley Hopkins (1844–89) he did not invent his own metres but experimented with numerous conventional ones. Donald Davie (b.1922) has compared this interest with the Victorian engineers' concern with structure and it is true that Hardy's metres can be too mechanical and rigid.* He sometimes designed abstract metres first and later poured a poem, as it were, into the rigid, pre-designed mould. However, this constant experimentation did bring its rewards. He preferred to view metre and rhythm not as an engineer but from the standpoint of his first profession as an architect. In *The Life of Thomas Hardy* he wrote:

> That the author loved the art of concealing art was undiscerned. For instance, as to rhythm. Years earlier he had decided that too regular a beat was bad art. . . . He knew that in architecture cunning irregularity is of enormous worth, and it is obvious that he carried on into his verse, perhaps in part unconsciously, the Gothic art-principle in which he had been trained—the principle of spontaneity found in mouldings, tracery, and such like—resulting in the 'unforeseen' (as it has been called) character of his metres and stanzas, that of stress rather than of syllable, poetic texture rather than poetic veneer; the latter kind of thing, under the name of 'constructed ornament', being what he, in common with every Gothic student, had been taught to avoid as the plague (pp.300–1).

Hardy alters rhythm by changing the number of syllables in a line. The number of stresses is constant but their effect is changed, as in 'Weathers': 'And the little brown nightingale bills his best' compared with 'And hill-hid tides throb, throe on throe'. Occasionally, Hardy will add or substract a stress from the established pattern in order to achieve a particular effect, as the added stress in the last line of 'Neutral Tones'

* In *Thomas Hardy and British Poetry*, Routledge & Kegan Paul, London, 1973, Ch. I.

hammers home the desolate symbols of lost love. Hardy's subtle use of caesura has been commented on several times. The two verses quoted in the last section from 'The Man He Killed' show how effectively he used metrical pauses to convey normal speech. Frequently the metre and rhythm reinforce meaning by their unobtrusiveness. The simple but skilfully handled ballad metre of 'The Darkling Thrush' adds to its direct, sincere tone; there is no 'poetic veneer', no 'constructed ornament' to come between the reader and the stark nature of Hardy's vision. A notable exception to this restrained manner, which is effective partly by contrast with Hardy's usual practice, is the final verse of 'The Voice' where the poet's anguished state is reflected by the complete breakdown of the metre.

Conclusion

It is ultimately impossible to separate Hardy's subject-matter from his poetic method, the content from the form, the analysis of what he says from how he says it. We appear to separate the two at times for easier explanation, but the separation is largely a matter of critical convenience and an attempt has been made throughout Part 3 to explain form in terms of content. For instance, we have seen that Hardy's diction is mixed and his imagery verbal because this alone could convey his view of life. Similarly, he uses irony and dramatic narrative because they enable him to present the mysterious, often sad events of life in a structured way within the framework of his beliefs and doubts.

This may help to explain what Hardy is saying and how he says it, and the interrelationship between the two, but perhaps it still fails to account fully for the emotional effect of a poem. A poem refers to objects and experiences in life outside itself and at the same time is a formal object and an experience in its own right. How does this object succeed in evoking emotion in the reader? T.S. Eliot personally disliked Hardy's work, but his well-known statement can be applied to Hardy's poetry:

> The only way of expressing emotion in the form of art is by finding an 'objective correlative'; in other words, a set of objects, a situation, a chain of events which shall be the formula of that *particular* emotion; such that when the external facts, which must terminate in sensory experience, are given, the emotion is immediately evoked.*

This process can be very clearly seen at work in the early poem 'Neutral Tones'. Hardy begins by presenting 'a set of objects, a situation, a chain of events'—a pond on a winter's day, the pale sun, a few grey leaves on the ground, the changing face of the woman. In the final verse, these

*F. Kermode (ed.), *Selected Prose of T.S. Eliot*, Faber, London, 1975, p.48.

objects and events become the 'objective correlative' for Hardy of the pain of love:

> Since then, keen lessons that love deceives,
> And wrings with wrong, have shaped to me
> Your face, and the God-curst sun, and a tree,
> And a pond edged with greyish leaves.

In other words, the scene has become a symbol that stands for the pain of love. It no longer records, as in verse I, a particular, personal event, but has become generalised to a symbol of an emotion common to all mankind. It is 'the formula of that *particular* emotion' which when recounted evokes the emotion.

The analogy of poetry with a scientific formula may seem reductive, but it does help us to understand Hardy's poetic method. Critics have frequently been baffled by the way in which Hardy's poetry seems so simple yet is capable of evoking a profound emotional response. Much of the conventional apparatus of criticism, the analysis of complex ideas, the cross-referencing with literary influences and movements, the search for subtle ambiguities, is largely irrelevant with Hardy's poetry. In the past, this misled critics into regarding Hardy as a sort of self-educated rustic who clumsily blundered into moments of greatness. Now we have more respect for Hardy's intellect and careful craftsmanship, but critics still show themselves somewhat baffled by Hardy's achievement when they finally resort to referring to his 'sincerity', 'honesty' and 'humanity'. These terms by themselves are not very helpful in explaining his aesthetic achievement, though any account that fails to include them would be seriously inadequate.

In the final analysis, Hardy's achievement lies in his ability to find the 'objective correlative' to life's emotions and to evoke these emotions in the reader. He does this by presenting a dramatic chain of events, usually of an ironic nature, that stands as a symbol for the emotion. 'Neutral Tones' is a particularly clear and uncommonly static example of this symbolising power which helps us to see why the Imagist poet Ezra Pound (1885–1972) admired the 'clarity' of Hardy's verse.* Usually the symbolising power is of a more dramatic nature with a longer perspective between past events and present meditation on them. The emotion may be sorrow for the loss of the unreflecting joy of childhood, as in 'The Self-Unseeing'; or for the loss of unreflecting faith, as in 'The Oxen'; or for the transitory nature of all things, as in 'During Wind and Rain'.

The most developed theme is the loss of love and its recall through memory in the 'Poems of 1912–13', and it is here that we actually witness the poetic process in action as Hardy painfully but finally triumphantly

* D. Paige (ed.), *The Letters of Ezra Pound*, Faber, New York, 1951, p.386.

achieves his complex, symbolising chain of events by reactivating his memories in contact with 'old love's domain'. This involves facing the degree of loss in the present but affirming the positive value of the experience of love and its memory:

> Primaeval rocks from the road's steep border,
>   And much have they faced there, first and last,
> Of the transitory in Earth's long order;
>   But what they record in colour and cast
>   Is—that we two passed.

A particular past event, at a particular place, is gathered up into the present and represents that complex of emotions that includes love, the loss of love and the memory of it. Such are Hardy's 'moments of vision', common emotions experienced by all men, caught up from the flux of time and held in defiance of it until the final oblivion of death. F.R. Leavis recognised his approach and why it impresses with its deep sincerity and rugged honesty:

> ... the single-minded integrity of his pre-occupation with a real world and a real past, the intentness of his focus upon particular facts and situations, gives this poetry the solidest kind of emotional substance. There is no emotionality. The emotion seems to inhere in the reality recognised and grasped.*

Although Hardy relentlessly probes the darker mysteries of life, he is seldom a depressing or enervating poet to read. It is not just that he is capable of moments of pure lyric joy, as in 'When I Set Out for Lyonnesse', or of celebrating the robust pleasures of life, as in 'Great Things', but that his poetry affirms life in describing and evoking its deepest emotions, even though these emotions blend sorrow with joy. He may often be pessimistic about the nature of the universe and man's place in it, but he is never cynical or negative about the nature of man. He wrote that human nature is 'neither ghastly, hateful, nor ugly; neither commonplace, unmeaning, nor tame, but ... slighted and enduring, and withal singularly colossal and mysterious'.† It is the depth of Hardy's compassion for human nature that caused him to mourn its suffering and, as Lord David Cecil has written, '... his tragic sense comes from the tension he feels between his sense of man's capacity for joy and his realisation that this is all too often disastrously thwarted.'‡ Although Hardy's vision is a sorrowing one, his poetry is an unpretentious and loving account of ordinary life, and the prevailing mood is not of gloom but of compassion and gentleness.

* 'Hardy the Poet', pp.94–5.
† Quoted by C. Day Lewis, 'The Lyrical Poetry' in *Thomas Hardy: Poems*, p.154.
‡ 'The Hardy Mood' in *Thomas Hardy: Poems*, p.235.

Part 4

Hints for study

WHEN YOU ARE EXAMINED on Hardy's poetry, the examiners are looking for your intelligent response to the poetry, and it has been the aim of these notes to help you towards such a response. This section is designed to help you communicate your response in an examination, and this is best achieved by looking at the type of questions you are likely to be asked, analysing them and developing an approach to answering them. Here are four questions taken from Oxford and Cambridge GCE Advanced Level papers:

(1) How would you reply to a critic who said that Hardy's use of words in his poetry was 'insensitive'?
(2) 'Many of Hardy's poems seem awkward and halting.' Is this necessarily a flaw in his technique? Base your answer on analyses of any *two* or *three* poems.
(3) 'His poems express a sense of the irreconcilable disparity between the way things ought to be and the way they are.' Discuss this view of Hardy's poetry.
(4) Which of the poems of Hardy that you have read do you consider to be the most characteristic of the poet, and why?

The first point is that you must read the questions very carefully, analysing every word in them. If we take the four questions given above, the first thing we should notice is that they fall into two broad categories—the first two focus on style, the second two on content. The categorisation is general because they are not exclusively about style or content, and, as we saw in Part 3, the two are inseparably interrelated, but it is very useful to understand where the main focus of a question is directed in order to see what sort of answer the examiner is expecting from you.

A second point is that the examiner is asking you for your opinion on the poems and he expects you to state an articulate case or argument, and this means supporting your argument with appropriate examples from the poetry. The examiner is not so much interested in your general knowledge of Hardy's poetry as in your response to it and your ability to communicate this response intelligently. It is therefore seldom appropriate to quote a whole verse or give a précis of a poem; the examiner is more interested in your opinions and your ability to back them up by appropriate references. Questions 1 and 2 will need a good number of specific references to prove your points about Hardy's use of words, his rhymes and rhythms. You will need to concentrate on single words, phrases and sentences extending over several lines, but you will not be expected to quote more than two or three lines at a stretch. Questions 3 and 4 will probably involve more references to poems by title, but note that Question 4 will demand a detailed knowledge of the poems that you select as the most characteristic. It is a good general rule to refer to a poem and usually to quote from it for every point you make.

Clearly this is going to demand a good deal of preparation before the examination. The best form of preparation is to practise the types of question you are likely to be asked and prepare a good number of specific points about the poetry with appropriate references and quotations. These points will be the building-blocks from which you can construct an answer to any type of question you may be asked. You will need points with quotations on both style and content, and you must be prepared to change points around, to choose some and reject others, in planning your answer.

Assuming you have done this preparation before the examination, you should follow these three stages when you are actually in the examination room:

(1) Analyse the question
(2) Decide on your approach
(3) Plan your essay with appropriate references and quotations.

The necessity for these preliminary stages before writing cannot be emphasised too much. Many an examination has been failed not because the student was ignorant of his subject or could not express himself but because he rushed at the questions, misreading them and failing to organise his thoughts into a coherent answer.

Model answers to questions

Let us now take four questions and prepare answers for them, beginning with Question 1. Notice first of all that this question directs our answer to defending Hardy of the charge of insensitivity in his choice of words. The essay that follows is not the 'right' answer because one person will always disagree to a certain extent with another person on matters of opinion, and literary criticism is not purely factual but involves value judgements and opinions. It is, however, vital that you should be accurate in matters of fact and well informed in matters of opinion which you must be able to defend by the use of appropriate references and quotations.

---

1. How would you reply to a critic who said that Hardy's use of words in his poetry was 'insensitive'?

Hardy's poetry often has a rough-hewn quality in its use of words, as in these lines from 'An Unkindly May':

> The sun frowns whitely in eye-trying flaps
> Through passing cloud-holes, mimicking audible taps.

The first line is a fine description of Hardy's characteristically pale sun, but the stress placed on the clumsy 'mimicking audible taps' does not seem to be warranted by the sense; it adds nothing to the poem to describe the sun as pretending to make tapping noises. Frequently, however, what appears at first sight as an awkward oddity, is revealed on closer reading to be an effective use of words, embodying what Hardy admired in Barnes's poetry, his 'closeness of phrase to his vision'.

It is not difficult to dispel the old myth of Hardy the rustic, self-taught writer stumbling accidentally on greatness. The revisions to his poetry reveal a highly self-conscious artist. For instance, the manuscript version of the last line of the second verse of 'The Voice' reads: 'Even to the original hat and gown!'. The word 'original' is odd, but Hardy made the line even odder by printing it as 'Even to the original air-blue gown!'. This brilliantly conveys Emma's reality, caught in the bright picture of her wearing a gown of a particular colour, the 'original' one of her lover's memory. By contrast the 'hat and gown' is too generalised to portray a vivid image of a real, felt presence; and that is the main purpose of this verse in a poem that is dealing with the poet's anguished conflict about the reality of Emma as a potent, consoling memory. Another example of Hardy's accurate use of words is found in 'Beeny Cliff':

> O the opal and the sapphire of that wandering western sea,
> And the woman riding high above with bright hair flapping free.

These are unusual instances of the 'jewelled line' in poetry that Hardy said he instinctively avoided yet could write when, as here, he deliberately wished to convey a romantic image. But even here, Hardy's characteristic focus on the actual causes him to select the odd word 'flapping' when a more 'jewelled' word, still retaining the alliteration, would have been 'flowing'. 'Flapping' is the better word, conveying real hair on a real woman without upsetting the general romantic image. The reader feels that Hardy really observed that hair and that the word accurately describes Emma's luxurious curls. Numerous other examples of Hardy's handling of words could be given. For instance, from 'After a Journey':

Ignorant of what there is flitting here to see,
The waked birds preen and the seals flop lazily.

The somewhat onomatopoeic word 'flop' exactly conveys the physical action of seals and sets up a telling contrast between their careless, natural ignorance and the haunted poet's tensed awareness of the ghost in his mind.

However, the critic who claims that Hardy's use of words is 'insensitive' may have in mind what Leavis called the 'gauche unshrinking mismarriage—group mismarriages—of his diction'.* It is true that Hardy often clashes different levels of diction, but he does so for a purpose. For instance, 'And There Was a Great Calm' begins with the abstractions of 'Passion', 'Despair' and the 'Spirit of Pity'. It moves from this elevated level to the colloquial level of 'dug-outs', 'snipers' and 'Huns'; the conversational 'Strange, this! How? All firing stopped?'; and the question framed in biblical language:

'Will men some day be given to grace? yea, wholly,
And in good sooth, as our dreams used to run?'

Finally the poem returns to the original question of the 'Spirit of Pity': 'Why?'. This is not clumsiness but a deliberate way of broadening the range of questions asked about war. Similarly, in 'To an Unborn Pauper Child' Hardy begins the poem by conveying the awesome dangers that beset the child in terms of the inhuman abstractions that rule the world:

The Doomsters heap
Travails and teens around us here,
And Time-wraiths turn our songsingings to fear.

This contrasts movingly with the biblical, rather archaic but mono-syllabic diction of verse V, where Hardy expresses his human compassion for the child doomed to enter such a world:

Fain would I, dear, find some shut plot
Of earth's wide wold for thee ...

One of Hardy's most effective shifts in the level of diction occurs in 'In Time of "The Breaking of Nations"' where the simple diction of the first two verses contrasts with the heightened, archaic diction of the last verse. The effect of this shift is to elevate love, the 'maid and her wight', above both the destructiveness of war and the monotony of labour.

Hardy deliberately rejected the poetic decorum of the Victorians, the unwritten code whereby it was agreed that certain words and subjects were inherently 'poetic', others 'prosaic', and some not suitable to appear in writing at all—like the abortion in 'A Sunday Morning

* 'Hardy the Poet', p.88.

Tragedy' or the prostitution in 'The Ruined Maid'. Hardy rejected this because he felt that the old faith and way of life that was reflected in this decorum had been swept away by modern science. Man was alone with the painful accident of his consciousness in a world that possessed no meaning beyond what he could impose on it. In such a situation the poet must seize all levels of language in his attempt to make sense of the world, to attain 'closeness of phrase to his vision', from the conventionally 'poetic' of 'Yonder a maid and her wight' to the modern, as in the car that 'whangs' past in 'Nobody Comes'. These levels have a force by their historic or present associations which Hardy can use for effect by clashing or contrasting them, as he does in 'In Time of "The Breaking of Nations"'. But essentially the richness of Hardy's diction reflects the end of the order that sustained the different levels, opening the whole of the language for the poet's use in his search to bring about a new sense of order within the poem. Hence, Hardy's use of words is frequently highly idiosyncratic, even odd, but invariably it conveys his meaning precisely and is a major element in giving his poetry that sense of a man sincerely striving to record facts and emotions faithfully.

Question 2 invites us to qualify the apparently negative comment of the critic quoted, to find some positive qualities in what is awkward and halting in Hardy's poetry. Notice also that we are required to write on 'any *two* or *three* poems', so we must choose our poems with care to illustrate the points we wish to make. Once again, it would be impossible to answer this question without a *detailed* knowledge of some of Hardy's poems.

---

2. Many of Hardy's poems seem awkward and halting. Is this necessarily a flaw in his technique? Base your answers on analyses of any *two* or *three* poems.

The extent of the 'awkward and halting' in Hardy's poetry can be greatly exaggerated. There are many fine poems, often in simple ballad metre, such as 'The Oxen', where the rhythms of the verse flow without any awkwardness. On the other hand, there are poems such as 'After a Journey', where the metre is more complex and the rhythms change from flowing to halting for deliberate effect. For instance, the last lines of the poem reflect the natural rhythms of relaxed speech, moving towards the joyful final two lines:

> Trust me, I mind not, though Life lours,
>   The bringing me here; nay, bring me here again!
>   I am just the same as when
> Our days were a joy, and our paths through flowers.

Contrast this with verse II, which is deliberately hesitant in rhythm, reflecting the difficulty Hardy finds in talking about his past with Emma:

> What have you now found to say of our past—
>   Scanned across the dark space wherein I have lacked you?
> Summer gave us sweets, but autumn wrought division?
>   Things were not lastly as firstly well
>   With us twain, you tell?

This has the awkwardness of the tentative rhythms of apology.

The best example of this deliberate awkwardness when referring to his past with Emma occurs in another of Hardy's finest poems, 'The Voice'. The complexity of the syntax of the first verse makes it very hard to understand on first reading, and the effect of this is to convey Hardy's reticence in discussing the subject, and to conceal the suggestion of blaming Emma for having 'changed from the one who was all to me'. The emphasis is shifted to 'when our day was fair'. Then in verse II, where Hardy becomes increasingly confident that he does see and hear Emma, the rhythm of the verse becomes easier. In the final verse, where he expresses an anguished state of doubt about the possibility of recapturing her memory, the metre breaks down altogether. The poem itself enacts his faltering.

Another notable example of the skilful use of contorted syntax occurs in 'A Broken Appointment'. Apart from two apt neologisms, 'hope-hour' and 'time-torn', the diction is very straightforward. There is only one metaphor, 'marching Time', fairly conventional but establishing an important theme in the poem. Yet the first verse is not easy to decode, mainly because of the syntax which delays the main clause 'Grieved I' until the penultimate line. The calculated effect of this is to shift the emphasis from Hardy's selfish grief that she has not kept her appointment with him, and place it on his altruistic sense of grief that he has found his love lacking in 'high compassion' and 'lovingkindness'. The second verse, which acknowledges that she does not love him but nevertheless asserts that she should have kept the appointment to 'soothe a time-torn man', is written with appropriately confident rhythms and more direct syntax. Once again, what is halting and awkward reflects the naturally hesitant rhythms of grief, while the more confident rhythms reflect the overcoming of grief.

The three poems discussed in this essay are generally acknowledged to be among Hardy's finest. It is quite clear that he is fully in control of the diction, rhythm and syntax of the poems because he can alter them to reflect the changing meaning of the poems. When he writes in an awkward or halting manner he creates a very idiosyncratic and moving 'grammar of grief'.

3. 'His poems express a sense of the irreconcilable disparity between the way things ought to be and the way they are.' Discuss this view of Hardy's poetry.

A constant theme of Hardy's poetry is expressed in his poem 'Yell'ham-Wood's Story': 'Life offers—to deny!'. For instance, 'During Wind and Rain' is constructed out of images of life systematically juxtaposed with images of death. Each verse presents a vivid picture of a family building its collective life in a spirit of harmony and joy. This is interrupted in the penultimate line of each verse by the lyrical refrain which shifts the scenes of joy into the past. The present is described in the last line of each verse with an ominous image of death culminating in the final line of the poem, 'Down their carved names the rain-drop ploughs'. Characteristically, Hardy views the joys of the past from the standpoint of a sorrowing present. The mood is elegiac; it does not deny the joys of life but mourns the inevitability of their passing.

This is essentially an ironic view of life, in the broadest sense of ironic. Sometimes the irony is explicitly on a cosmic level, as in 'Convergence of the Twain'. Man constructs a mighty ship, a reflection of his pride and intended to pander to pride and luxury. At the same time, the 'Immanent Will':

> Prepared a sinister mate
> For her—so gaily great—
> A Shape of ice, for the time far and dissociate.

At the command of the 'Spinner of the Years', iceberg and ship collide, 'And consummation comes, and jars two hemispheres'. The sexual metaphor of 'consummation' is in itself ironic as the mating brings death, not life. The poem raises, but does not answer, questions about the nature of the universe, though it suggests that the universe is ruled by a malevolent force.

Occasionally, the ironies of life can suggest to Hardy the opposite, that perhaps there is a benevolent force. In 'The Darkling Thrush', it is the ironic contrast between the desolate reality of nature in midwinter, paralleling Hardy's own sense of inner emptiness, and the extra-ordinarily joyful song of the frail thrush that prompts him to ponder on the possibility of 'Hope'. He wonders if the song has significance just because there is 'So little cause for carolings'. Joy certainly exists in the bird's song and possibly 'Hope' also, though Hardy remains 'unaware' of it as a personal experience in this and most of his poems. Hardy expresses the reality of joy in 'Great Things' where he celebrates the pleasures of cider, dancing and love. In the final verse, he character-istically foresees the end of joy in death, though he refuses to allow this to deny the importance of life's pleasures.

It is in the 'Poems of 1912–13' that Hardy most movingly explores the problem of life's promise and the blighting of this promise in the juxtaposition of his youthful love with Emma, their long years of unhappiness, her sudden death that prevented reconciliation, and his attempt to recapture their lost love. As a series, the poems represent the working through of Hardy's central concern, a type of Hardy myth. It begins with the despairing anguish of 'The Going' and its fear of the impossibility of consolation; works through the problem of establishing a new relationship with Emma and recapturing his memories in poems such as 'The Voice'; and culminates in the triumph of 'After a Journey' where he achieves his desire of holding his love and Emma herself alive in his memory, defying 'Time's derision':

> I am just the same as when
> Our days were a joy, and our paths through flowers.

This is the nearest Hardy ever came to reconciling himself to the death of love, to loss and sorrow; but the true ending of the series is not on this almost ecstatic note but in the more typical, quieter mood of resignation of 'At Castle Boterel'. Hardy's achievement is secure—the memory of Emma and their love is powerful, and it asserts the value of moments of intense human experience over indifferent nature and 'Times unflinching rigour':

> It filled but a minute. But was there ever
>   A time of such quality, since or before,
> In that hill's story? To one mind never ...

Yet this is 'To one mind' only, and as he admits in the final verse, death will eventually erase his memories:

>   ... for my sand is sinking,
> And I shall traverse old love's domain
>   Never again.

Hardy found no permanent way to reconcile himself to the facts of loss of love, sorrow and death. Although he earnestly studied philosophy, he discovered no system of belief to replace his loss of faith in Christianity. Occasionally he seems to have thought of the universe as a malevolent place, as in 'Convergence of the Twain'. More commonly, the 'Immanent Will' is an indifferent, mechanical force. Very rarely, Hardy can entertain the thought that hope might exist, as in 'The Darkling Thrush'. But his most consistent mood is expressed in the 'Poems of 1912–13' where man is viewed as a lonely figure, amid a nature indifferent to his feelings, struggling to maintain his sense of love and joy, yet ultimately doomed by death to oblivion. There can be no lasting reconciliation in this sombre vision between man's capacity for joy and the inevitability of its destruction. Yet, Hardy's poetry is seldom gloomy or depressing because he valued life so highly, depicted its joys so vividly and struggled so earnestly to affirm their value in the face of what he regarded as an indifferent universe. His tragic sense and the pathos of his poems arise precisely out of his keen awareness of that 'disparity between the way things ought to be and the way they are'.

Question 4 was 'Which of the poems of Hardy that you have read do you consider to be the most characteristic of the poet, and why?'. If you reconsider the answer given to Question 3, you will realise that it could be changed to provide an answer to Question 4 by developing the section on the 'Poems of 1912–13' as Hardy's most characteristic. A good case could be made for some other poems, but the 'Poems of 1912–13' provide a series of poems focusing intently on Hardy's deepest concerns. You should notice that an answer to one question often provides a partial answer to another. This is what is meant by referring to your preparation for an examination as the accumulation of building-blocks of ideas plus references on the poems. These building-blocks are not only useful for one particular essay but can be rearranged to construct other essays.

Consider the list of further questions given below. Most of them can be answered partially, or even completely, from the building-blocks that were used for Questions 1–3. This is not always immediately apparent. You will have to think carefully about each question, referring back to the poems themselves and to the relevant sections of these notes.

(5) 'Hardy is, above all, the poet of man's mortality, of the passing away of things.' Discuss this view of Hardy's poetry.
(6) Discuss the importance of irony in Hardy's poetry.
(7) How did Hardy's loss of faith in Christianity affect his poetry?
(8) F.R. Leavis said that Hardy made a 'style out of stylelessness'. What did he mean, and do you agree?
(9) Hardy said he admired the 'closeness of phrase to his vision' in the poetry of William Barnes. Do you think Hardy achieved this in his own poetry?
(10) Hardy wrote, 'An ample theme: the intense interests, passions, and strategy that throb through the commonest lives' (*The Life*, p.153). Does his poetry illustrate this?

---

10. Hardy wrote, 'An ample theme: the intense interests, passions, and strategy that throb through the commonest lives'. Does his poetry illustrate this?

Hardy speaks with various poetic voices; one of them is the philosophical, public voice of 'Convergence of the Twain' on the occasion of an international disaster. Although the ironical perspective and the style of this poem are typical of Hardy, this is not the poetic voice that we normally associate with him. Hardy's mind often works with abstractions such as the 'Immanent Will', but he seldom writes a poem so lacking in compassionate concern for humanity, and it is this concern which is the essential hallmark of his most characteristic voice.

Most of Hardy's occasional poems contain the humane element. 'And There Was a Great Calm', written 'On the Signing of the Armistice, 11 Nov. 1918', may begin with abstractions such as the 'Spirit of Pity' and 'Despair', but the body of the poem is concerned with the questions raised by 'the bereft, and meek, and lowly', by the common soldier of either side, and even by 'the mute bird' and 'worn horses'. It is wholly characteristic of Hardy that his war poems focus not on abstract ideas such as patriotism or the nation but on the ordinary person tragically caught up in a senseless experience—the wives in 'The Going of the Battery', the common soldier in 'The Man He Killed', and the simple young countryman in 'Drummer Hodge'. It is of no matter what 'side' these people are on. In the broader perspective of 'In Time of "The Breaking of Nations"', war and dynasties are seen as insignificant compared with the eternal verities of labour and love—the 'man harrowing clods' and the 'maid and her wight'.

Hardy's compassionate eye always sought for the significant in lives that might appear insignificant. He valued the quiet pride of the man in 'The Old Workman' who, although he is injured by his work and unknown to those he has worked for, is proud that he has created something that will keep people 'safe from harm, and right and tight', something that is firm enough to outlive him, a monument to his good workmanship. Hardy celebrates a similar spirit in the poem 'A Man' where a workman refuses to demolish a beautiful old house, 'wrecking what our age cannot replace'. His principles cost him dear and he dies poor and workless, but Hardy comments that he longs to hold:

> As truth what fancy saith:
> 'His protest lives where deathless things abide!'

Often the countryman's love of a strange tale attracts Hardy to the tragic, frequently ironic experiences of ordinary people, such as in 'A Sunday Morning Tragedy', based on a true story, where the mother's attempt to abort her daughter's illegitimate baby leads to the girl's death on the very day her lover announces his intention of marrying her. There are numerous ballads based on strange local Dorset tales about ordinary people, such as 'The Choirmaster's Burial', 'The Paphian Ball', and 'The Dance at the Phoenix'. Yet, Hardy can be at his most moving when he writes about very common experiences which he renders into something vitally significant, as in 'A Broken Appointment' where there is typically no self-pity but a transformation of personal grief into a plea for human compassion and 'lovingkindness'. This poetic power to discern the significant in the apparently insignificant extends to the animal world and even to inanimate nature. 'Afterwards' is such a moving personal elegy because of the intentness of Hardy's concern for the 'innocent creatures' and his protectiveness towards the humble and meek. He was particularly open to the mystery of life, from 'the full-starred heavens that winter sees' in 'Afterwards', to the insects in 'An August Midnight':

> 'God's humblest, they!' I muse. Yet why?
> They know Earth-secrets that know not I.

This alertness to life in all its forms, especially to the significance and mystery of ordinary life, makes Hardy's poetry immediately accessible to the reader. We are engaged directly by poetry that is concerned with 'the intense interests, passions, and strategy that throb through the commonest lives'. For instance, in 'Neutral Tones' Hardy says that the pain of love is symbolised for him by common objects:

> Your face, and the God-curst sun, and a tree,
> And a pond edged with greyish leaves.

These objects are quite ordinary in verse 1, but in the final verse they have become stark images of the pain of love, symbols that transmit his emotion to the reader. Similarly, in 'During Wind and Rain' the family could represent any lively family engaged in normal activities. Against this are set archetypal images of death—leaves falling, storm-birds, the rotten rose, the rain on the tombstone. The juxtaposition of these common images of life and death generates the pathos of the poem, conveying a sense of the sadness of man's mortal nature and the inevitability of the passing of all his joys. Even the intensely personal 'Poems of 1912–13' achieve this universal significance because Hardy is able to draw from personal, often small incidents, general statements about remorse, love and death that apply to all men. It is this ability to express common emotions and portray the common human condition with such compassion that is Hardy's greatest poetic achievement.

Part 5

Suggestions for further reading

Texts

GIBSON, JAMES: *Chosen Poems of Thomas Hardy*, Macmillan Educational, London, 1975. This is the best selection of Hardy's poetry for the student. There is a useful introductory section, a rather short but discerning slection of the poems, with glossaries of obscure words and some notes.

Larger selections can be found in:

CREIGHTON, T.R.M.: *Poems of Thomas Hardy: A New Selection*, Macmillan, London, Revised edition 1977.
WRIGHT, DAVID: *Thomas Hardy: Selected Poems*, Penguin Books, Harmondsworth, 1978.

For the standard volume of all the poems see:

GIBSON, JAMES: *The Complete Poems of Thomas Hardy*, The New Wessex Edition, Macmillan, London, 1976.

Any student who enjoys the poetry will also enjoy Hardy's novels, all of which are published by Macmillan, London, in the hardback New Wessex Edition and in paperback.

Critical studies

BAILEY, J.O.: *The Poetry of Thomas Hardy: A Handbook and Commentary*, University of North Carolina Press, Chapel Hill, 1970. A useful and comprehensive reference book on all the poems, richer in biographical detail than critical comment.
GIBSON, J., and JOHNSON, T. (EDS.) *Thomas Hardy: Poems* (Casebook Series), Macmillan, London, 1979. A most useful collection of contemporary reviews of the poetry and critical essays up to 1975.
GITTINGS, ROBERT: *Young Thomas Hardy*, Heinemann, London, 1975.
GITTINGS, ROBERT: *The Older Hardy*, Heinemann, London, 1977. These two books are the most authoritative biography of Hardy and are very readable. They are also published by Penguin Books, Harmondsworth.

GUERARD, ALBERT J. (ED.): *Hardy: A Collection of Critical Essays* (Twentieth Century Views), Prentice-Hall, New Jersey, 1963. Contains three essays on the poems, one by W.H.Auden.

HARDY, EVELYN and GITTINGS, ROBERT (EDS.): *Some Recollections By Emma Hardy*, Oxford University Press, Oxford, 1979. After Emma's death, Hardy discovered that she had written a lively and vivid account of their meeting and courtship in Cornwall. These recollections helped to inspire him to write some of his finest love poems, notably the 'Poems of 1912–13'. Several poems, including some not in James Gibson's *Chosen Poems*, are printed in the book illustrating how Hardy was influenced by Emma's recollections and even in some cases adopted her words and phrases.

HYNES, SAMUEL: *The Pattern of Hardy's Poetry*, University of North Carolina Press, Chapel Hill, 1961. An interesting book-length study, concentrating on the structure of the poems.

MARSDEN, KENNETH: *The Poems of Thomas Hardy*, Athlone Press, London, 1969. Still perhaps the best general book-length study.

PINION, F.B.: *A Hardy Companion*, Macmillan, London, 1968. A useful book of general reference on both the novels and the poems.

The author of these notes

ROGER ELLIOTT was educated at Exeter College, Oxford and University College, Cardiff. He has taught in adult education in Sweden and at the University of Sokoto, Nigeria, and is now Lecturer in English at the United Nations Institute for Namibia, Lusaka, Zambia. He has written on environmental issues for Friends of the Earth, on the English language in Nigeria, and he is author of the York Notes on *Selected Poems of Andrew Marvell*.

York Notes: list of titles

CHINUA ACHEBE
Things Fall Apart

EDWARD ALBEE
Who's Afraid of Virginia Woolf?

MARGARET ATWOOD
The Handmaid's Tale

W. H. AUDEN
Selected Poems

JANE AUSTEN
Emma
Mansfield Park
Northanger Abbey
Persuasion
Pride and Prejudice
Sense and Sensibility

SAMUEL BECKETT
Waiting for Godot

ARNOLD BENNETT
The Card

JOHN BETJEMAN
Selected Poems

WILLIAM BLAKE
Songs of Innocence, Songs of Experience

ROBERT BOLT
A Man For All Seasons

CHARLOTTE BRONTË
Jane Eyre

EMILY BRONTË
Wuthering Heights

BYRON
Selected Poems

GEOFFREY CHAUCER
The Clerk's Tale
The Franklin's Tale
The Knight's Tale
The Merchant's Tale
The Miller's Tale
The Nun's Priest's Tale
The Pardoner's Tale
Prologue to the Canterbury Tales
The Wife of Bath's Tale

SAMUEL TAYLOR COLERIDGE
Selected Poems

JOSEPH CONRAD
Heart of Darkness

DANIEL DEFOE
Moll Flanders
Robinson Crusoe

SHELAGH DELANEY
A Taste of Honey

CHARLES DICKENS
Bleak House
David Copperfield
Great Expectations
Hard Times
Oliver Twist

EMILY DICKINSON
Selected Poems

JOHN DONNE
Selected Poems

DOUGLAS DUNN
Selected Poems

GERALD DURRELL
My Family and Other Animals

GEORGE ELIOT
Middlemarch
The Mill on the Floss
Silas Marner

T. S. ELIOT
Four Quartets
Murder in the Cathedral
Selected Poems
The Waste Land

WILLIAM FAULKNER
The Sound and the Fury

HENRY FIELDING
Joseph Andrews
Tom Jones

F. SCOTT FITZGERALD
The Great Gatsby
Tender is the Night

GUSTAVE FLAUBERT
Madame Bovary

E. M. FORSTER
Howards End
A Passage to India

JOHN FOWLES
The French Lieutenant's Woman

ELIZABETH GASKELL
North and South

WILLIAM GOLDING
Lord of the Flies

GRAHAM GREENE
Brighton Rock
The Heart of the Matter
The Power and the Glory

THOMAS HARDY
Far from the Madding Crowd
Jude the Obscure
The Mayor of Casterbridge
The Return of the Native
Selected Poems
Tess of the D' Urbervilles

L. P. HARTLEY
The Go-Between

NATHANIEL HAWTHORNE
The Scarlet Letter

SEAMUS HEANEY
Selected Poems

ERNEST HEMINGWAY
A Farewell to Arms
The Old Man and the Sea

SUSAN HILL
I'm the King of the Castle

HOMER
The Iliad
The Odyssey

GERARD MANLEY HOPKINS
Selected Poems

TED HUGHES
Selected Poems

ALDOUS HUXLEY
Brave New World

HENRY JAMES
The Portrait of a Lady

BEN JONSON
The Alchemist
Volpone

JAMES JOYCE
Dubliners
A Portrait of the Artist as a Young Man

JOHN KEATS
Selected Poems

PHILIP LARKIN
Selected Poems

D. H. LAWRENCE
The Rainbow
Selected Short Stories
Sons and Lovers
Women in Love

HARPER LEE
To Kill a Mockingbird

LAURIE LEE
Cider with Rosie

CHRISTOPHER MARLOWE
Doctor Faustus

ARTHUR MILLER
The Crucible
Death of a Salesman
A View from the Bridge

JOHN MILTON
Paradise Lost I & II
Paradise Lost IV & IX

SEAN O'CASEY
Juno and the Paycock

GEORGE ORWELL
Animal Farm
Nineteen Eighty-four

JOHN OSBORNE
Look Back in Anger

WILFRED OWEN
Selected Poems

HAROLD PINTER
The Caretaker

SYLVIA PLATH
Selected Works

ALEXANDER POPE
Selected Poems

J. B. PRIESTLEY
An Inspector Calls

WILLIAM SHAKESPEARE
Antony and Cleopatra
As You Like It
Coriolanus
Hamlet
Henry IV Part I
Henry IV Part II
Henry V
Julius Caesar
King Lear
Macbeth
Measure for Measure
The Merchant of Venice
A Midsummer Night's Dream
Much Ado About Nothing
Othello
Richard II
Richard III
Romeo and Juliet
Sonnets
The Taming of the Shrew
The Tempest

Troilus and Cressida
Twelfth Night
The Winter's Tale

GEORGE BERNARD SHAW
Arms and the Man
Pygmalion
Saint Joan

MARY SHELLEY
Frankenstein

PERCY BYSSHE SHELLEY
Selected Poems

RICHARD BRINSLEY SHERIDAN
The Rivals

R. C. SHERRIFF
Journey's End

JOHN STEINBECK
The Grapes of Wrath
Of Mice and Men
The Pearl

TOM STOPPARD
Rosencrantz and Guildenstern are Dead

JONATHAN SWIFT
Gulliver's Travels

JOHN MILLINGTON SYNGE
The Playboy of the Western World

W. M. THACKERAY
Vanity Fair

MARK TWAIN
Huckleberry Finn

VIRGIL
The Aeneid

DEREK WALCOTT
Selected Poems

ALICE WALKER
The Color Purple

JOHN WEBSTER
The Duchess of Malfi

OSCAR WILDE
The Importance of Being Earnest

THORNTON WILDER
Our Town

TENNESSEE WILLIAMS
The Glass Menagerie

VIRGINIA WOOLF
Mrs Dalloway
To the Lighthouse

WILLIAM WORDSWORTH
Selected Poems

W. B. YEATS
Selected Poems

York Handbooks: list of titles

YORK HANDBOOKS form a companion series to York Notes and are designed to meet the wider needs of students of English and related fields. Each volume is a compact study of a given subject area, written by an authority with experience in communicating the essential ideas to students at all levels.

AN A.B.C. OF SHAKESPEARE
by P. C. BAYLEY

A DICTIONARY OF BRITISH AND IRISH AUTHORS
by ANTONY KAMM

A DICTIONARY OF LITERARY TERMS (Second Edition)
by MARTIN GRAY

ENGLISH GRAMMAR
by LORETO TODD

ENGLISH POETRY
by CLIVE T. PROBYN

AN INTRODUCTION TO AUSTRALIAN LITERATURE
by TREVOR JAMES

AN INTRODUCTION TO LINGUISTICS
by LORETO TODD

AN INTRODUCTION TO LITERARY CRITICISM
by RICHARD DUTTON

AN INTRODUCTORY GUIDE TO ENGLISH LITERATURE
by MARTIN STEPHEN

THE METAPHYSICAL POETS
by TREVOR JAMES

PREPARING FOR EXAMINATIONS IN ENGLISH LITERATURE
by NEIL McEWAN

READING THE SCREEN: AN INTRODUCTION TO FILM STUDIES
by JOHN IZOD

STUDYING CHAUCER
by ELISABETH BREWER

STUDYING JANE AUSTEN
by IAN MILLIGAN

STUDYING SHAKESPEARE
by MARTIN STEPHEN *and* PHILIP FRANKS

STUDYING THOMAS HARDY
by LANCE ST JOHN BUTLER

WOMEN WRITERS IN ENGLISH LITERATURE
by JANE STEVENSON